Isabella Warrior Queen

- Michael G Kramer OMIEAust.

Author at Australian camp at Nui Dat S. Vietnam 1968

- ISBN = 978-0-6455-701-6-8

- Copyright © 2023

Book Titles by Michael G Kramer OMIEAust.

- Isabella Warrior Queen
- A Castle of Doomsday 2nd Edition
- A Gracious Enemy & After the War Volume 1
- A Gracious Enemy & After the War Volume 2
- Arminius & Thusnelda Versus Rome
- A Castle Of Doomsday
- A Gracious Enemy
- Anglo-Saxon Invasion
- Now What?!!
- For the Love of Armin
- Full Circle for Mick

Table of Contents

Preface	6
Forward	8
Introduction	8
King Henry III of England	9
Edward I 'Longshanks'	11
Bearing & Character of Edward …	11
Finance and Expulsion of the Jews	20
Prince Edward	23
Piers Gaveston	24
Isabella	27
Night of the Wedding	30
Coronation of Edward II & Isabella	32
Isabella & Edward Campaign Together	33
Confrontation at Leeds Castle	36
Edward Discusses Sexuality with Court	37
Edward & Gaveston Separate	40
Trial of Piers Gaveston	42
King Edward II is Devastated	46
Edward & Isabella First Child	47
A Loving Open Marriage?	49
A fire in the Bedroom	52
The Battle of Boroughbridge	53
Location of Boroughbridge Battlefield	56
The Battle is Nigh	57
The Trial of Baron Roger de Clifford	60
The Sentence	61
Le Despenser Family	64
Younger Le Despencer is King's …	66
Edward II is Once Again Queer	68
Isabella Hears & Sees Them	70
Edmund Fitzalan joins the younger …	74
The Bishop of Winchester Preaches	76
Roger's Escape from the Tower	78
1325 Isabella is Sent to Paris Negotiate	83
Isabella & Roger Mortimer Meet in Paris	87
Preparing for the Invasion	90

Edward II asks Isabella to Return	91
Bishop Orleton Preaches Against	97
1326 Isabella Invades England	102
Isabella Makes a Proclamation	105
The Despencers, Fitzalan & King flee	106
Soldiers Desert King Edward II	110
Isabella & Her Amy Besiege Bristol	114
Isabella Orders the Arrest of her	116
Parliament of the 7th of January 1327	122
The Teenage King Thinks he saw …	123
Edward III Overhears Plotting …	125
Isabella & Mortimer in Scotland	127
The Aftermath	132
Treaty of Edinburgh – Northampton	133
Terms of the Treaty	134
King Edward III Gathers Strength	135
The Captive Edward III sees His Father	137
Edward III Arrests his Tormentors	141
Isabella as Dowager Queen	147
Edward III's Letter Delivered	151
The Pope's Answer	153
At Six, Edward is called 'Black Prince'	154
Edward III claims the French Throne	155
Provocations!	157
The Edwardian War	159
The English Invasion of France	160
The 'Black Prince' Becomes Duke of …	161
English Action at Crecy	163
Siege of Calais	166
Amerigo of Pavia	168
Geoffrey de Charny	168
Informing Edward III	171
French Preparations	174
Battle for Calais	175
The Attack of Citadel Detachment	176
Main Force at Boulogne Gate of Calais	177
Events after the Battle of Calais	178
Financing the English Attack	182

Amerigo Returns to Serve English	184
Charny Commands French in the NE	184
Chivalry & National Identity	187
Cheshire Expedition	189
Campaign at Aquitaine	191
Battle of Poitiers	197
Black Prince Informed About French	201
The Black Prince Receives John II	204
Marriage of the Black Prince	205
Prince of Aquitaine & Gascony	206
Spanish Campaign	209
Burgos	219
War in Aquitaine 1366 – 1370	221
Return to England	224
Death of Edward the Black Prince	227
Transition - Dowager Princess of Wales	228
Summary	230
Bibliography	231

Michael G Kramer OMIEAust.

Preface

Warning – because the life of King Edward II had much to do with his male lovers, there are some love scenes between males. This novel is mainly about King Edward II, his wife Princess Isabella of France their children, and a grandson, but also, the relationship between Edward and two of his more well-known male lovers are examined in detail. So, if you are against people of the same sex having loving relationships, then perhaps this is not the book for you.

The tolerance of many governments and their agencies around world towards minority groups such as LGBTQI (Lesbian, Gay, Bi, Transition, Queer, Individual) communities is one of grudging acceptance in the countries and their states which allow their people to be part of that. (e.g. most of the western world).

However, that was not always the case. Even in Australia, as late as the mid-and-late1970s, homosexual men were prosecuted simply for being themselves. For example, in Sydney and all other Australian state capital cities, the police would go to where they knew that male homosexuals would be, and the police arrested the men for such things as *"Committing acts of indecency"*. There were also many other charges which could be used by police against the homosexual male community including the ages old charge of sodomy.

This book tells the story of Queen Isabella, her husband, and their children and their well-known grandson called *'The Black Prince'*. The simple truth of the matter is that King Edward II, who was the husband of Isabella and the father of her children, was in fact a bisexual man and a loving father, who was loved by and well-thought of by his own children.

However, during the time of the 14th century, those in power did not and could not differentiate between a man who was a bisexual man and one who was homosexual. Either a man was considered to be a normal or straight man or else society regarded him as a homosexual and called him a poofter. The influence of the Church at the time was such that the church condemned homosexual behaviour and the leaders of the Roman Catholic Church often took direct actions against homosexual males.

This story is about an amazing couple in the 14th century, who actually had a working *"Open Marriage"* such that Isabella even tolerated Edward II's homosexual activities with his male *"Favourites"*. Things remained that way for some time until one favourite of the king was killed, and he was replaced by Hugh Le Despenser the Younger. An intense homosexual affair developed between the King and his chamberlain. After some time, Hugh Le Despenser moved against Isabella by taking her children from her and that caused her to act against him and her husband after many other provocations.

Let us be open and frank here! I am a *Straight* man, but I do not impose my own sexuality upon others. If some-one wishes to be homosexual, bisexual, a lesbian, or any other form of *"Queer"*, that is their business and no-one else's! Because of the fact that I am straight, I have had to rely upon what I have heard and read about how the homosexuals made love.

Personally, I do not know. All the same, this book tries to address the sexuality of people whom others may call "Queer' or worse names.

All the same, I do realise that love between some males exists, just as it exists between some women. Thankfully, we all live in an age when people can live their lives as they choose, in the free western countries at least. No disrespect towards those who are *"Not Straight'* or who have either bisexual or homosexual tendencies is intended.

Forward

When the reviews of *A Castle of Doomsday* were being read by me, I was most impressed by a review from Peggy Wipf, who appears on Goodreads reviews as Pegboard and Amazon reviews as Jojo Maxson. In her review of my work, she stated *"... I think that this is just the beginning of Michael's historical fiction writing. He hinted as much. by saying. 'As there is so much more that could be written about Isabella and her supporters."*

So, moving right along, I hereby dedicate this novel to Peggy Wipf, Grymm Gevierre, Grady, and my other readers who have been so generous in their support of my writing. I also dedicate this novel to my supportive wife, Carolyn who has been my backstop from the beginning. So, Peggy, Grymm, Grady, my other readers and Carolyn, this book is for you! Enjoy!

Introduction

Gooday to you, honoured reader, I am the ghost of King Alfred the Great, I have looked down upon my former kingdom and I am appalled by the behaviour of many of those who are presently in power in my England. Because the history of England one of constant upheaval and fighting, this story shall begin with King Henry III. It is because I am now a ghost, that I can move forwards and backwards in time to explain some of the lessor known happenings which may interest you.

Also, no walls can hold me. These are the only advantages of being a ghost. I often yearn to eat and drink again, but on the plus side of things, I do not have to do so.

King Henry III of England

Henry was born on the 1st of October 1207, at the Great Hall, in Winchester, England. His mother, Isabella of Angoulême, had been in labour for some time and was uncomfortable with this birth. She began to dream during
her labours. After some time, her midwife called Margaret came to her. She said, *"Isabella, how is this birth going for you, are you comfortable or in pain?"* Isabella answered, *"What pain there is, I can easily bear. I have been getting dreams of this child. It is a boy, and I have had visions which are telling me that he will become the king after his father, John the First, but he will get a lot of problems from the barons who should always be supporting him. Instead, it looks like they will be in revolt and just try to take things in England for themselves!"* Margaret said, *"Oh, I see, so his reign may not be an easy one! What name shall he have?"* Isabella answered, *"Henry, he shall become Henry the Third of England!"*

The time quickly passed, and after ten years, the father of Henry (King John I) died, and that resulted in Henry III coming to the throne of England at the age of ten years. He ruled for the next fifty-six years until he died in 1272. unlike his father, King John I of England, he willing put his seal upon the great document we call Magna Carta. He set up the first Parliament because he needed the counsel of the barons, knights, and clerics on matters of law and taxation. And so, the stage was set for Parliament to slowly ebb away at royal power over the years, and finally become the democratic institution that is today.

In 1244 Henry was in conversation with his military and civilian advisors when a messenger arrived. The man was wearing chain-mail armour, and he appeared to be breathless. He was escorted into the throne-room and said, *"Your Majesty, the Scots are gathering and threatening to invade England! We must have better and more castles which are garrisoned and ready to use against the invaders, or we could lose this country!"*

Henry answered, *"I now authorise the immediate reconstruction of the entire York Castle, including its keep and motte at the ruins of York Castle. The other castle at Baile Hill in York will continue to be used for royal visits by myself. The work to be completed includes a towered curtain wall which shall surround York Castle and its Keep. It shall have a gatehouse of considerable size with two large towers. There shall also be a smaller gatehouse, and a small watergate into the city and a new stone Keep. The keep shall be of the quatrefoil design with four circular lobes.*

Each lobe shall measure 22 feet (6.5 metres) across, and the walls shall be nine (9) feet and six (6) inches (3 metres) thick. At its thickest, the tower shall be seventy-nine (79) feet (24 metres) There are to be defensive turrets between the lobes. I want large corbels and a central pier to support the weight of the stone and the first floor. Shooting points for cross-bows and long-bows are to be installed. A chapel is to be built over the entrance of the stone keep, and it shall measure fifteen (15) feet by fourteen (14) feet, and it will double as a portcullis chamber. The work shall be under the supervision of Master Mason Henry de Rayns, and the chief carpenter shall be Simon of Northampton."

The new castle needed constant maintenance and investment. The winter flooding of 1315 to 1316 caused subsidence of the motte and that required immediate repairs. During 1358–1360, the heavy keep again suffered from subsidence, causing the south-eastern lobe to crack from top to bottom. Meanwhile, King Henry III was succeeded by his son, Edward I, known as Edward Longshanks, the Hammer of the Scots!

Edward I "Longshanks-Hammer of the Scots"

Edward the First was born in 1239 and died in 1307. He reigned as King of England from 1272 to 1307, a reign of thirty-five years. During the 1250s the father of Edward, Henry III had attempted to control and dominate Wales using a series of military actions. They resulted in a series of costly defeats. The resulting negotiated peace gave Prince Llewelyn ap Gruffydd more territories in England.

Bearing and Character of Edward Longshanks

Physically, Edward was tall and had an athletic build. He was about six feet and two inches in height, His reputation was that of a fearless warrior with a quick and fierce temper who could explode into fury at the slightest provocation. That was one of the reasons that he was feared by many. Some people even called him a leopard. The reason? The leopard is a large cat which sizes up the situation before it strikes. Generally, a leopard will not strike unless it considers everything to be in its favour.

Soon after he assumed power from his father Henry III, Edward held his first Orders Group. He began proceedings by addressing the people present at his court. He said, *"Ladies and Gentlemen. We shall immediately set about the re-establishment of English law and order which has suffered badly because of mis-governing by my father, Henry III! There shall be an immediate and extensive change of most administrative personnel, and Robert Burnell is hereby appointed as Chancellor!"* That was carried out, and then Edward again spoke to his court.

He said, *"I am now replacing most of the officials of every locality in England such as the escheators and Sheriffs! This must be done because the current officials in these roles are clearly corrupt and serving their own interests! An extensive inquest shall be set in motion to hear all complaints about the abuse of royal power by royal government officers!*

This shall be the case even if it results in a new set of rolls per hundred (local government area). As well as that, I am going to recover all land and rights the crown has lost because of the reign of my father King Henry III. In order to challenge baronial rights, I shall enact the Statute of Westminster 1278 and the Statute of Gloucester 1278. These statutes shall allow a revival of the system of royal justices touring England in the performance of their duties!"

Edward went on to draw up laws concerning the family settlement of the land, the recovery of debts by merchants, and the settlement of disagreements and disputes.

Edward was an intelligent, aggressive warrior and an effective ruler who made full use of the Parliament to get his way. The simple fact about this is that Parliament met very infrequently if at all, and Edward found it easy to manipulate it.

Campaigning with his father against the enemies, Edward experienced the failures, and he determined not to make the same mistakes as his father. He was sitting on his throne when a messenger approached him. He was ushered into the presence of King Edward I. As the messenger approached the king, he spoke. The messenger said, *"Your Majesty, I have disturbing news for you from the Marcher Castles near the Welsh Border! Your barons and other lords have not been successful in collecting taxes from the Welsh, who refuse to pay. Not only that, but Prince Llewelyn also refuses to pay homage to you, Your Majesty!"*

Edward replied, *"By God and his Mother, I do not like what I am hearing! So, bloody Prince Llewelyn of the Welsh does not want to pay homage to me and is not paying his taxes! That is both an insult levelled directly at me and my England. Llewelyn and his cronies shall not get away this treasonous behaviour! An Orders Group shall be held here in my palace at mid-afternoon today, and all senior military and naval commanders are to attend. Orderly, you are to ensure that all commanders are informed of this immediately!"*

The King now spoke directly to the messenger who had delivered the news. He said, *"Messenger, you have done well, thank you for informing me of a grave situation. You may go to the Royal Kitchen, and both eat and drink your fill before you return to your duties. You are excused!"*

As the time of day progressed towards mid-afternoon, Edward's palace was filling with many men and their female companions. Edward addressed the military and naval officers and their female companions in his palace. He said, *"Ladies and Gentlemen, during this year of 1274, we are going to ensure that the Welsh and all others who do not toe the line or obey orders from England shall be invaded, defeated, and forced to pay homage to England, myself and our forces or I am not Edward!*

I have at hand a very large army of English cross-bow men, Long-bow archers, men-at-arms (infantry) and cavalry. After Llewellyn has been defeated, he shall be stripped of all of his territories! All of you who are members of my forces, are required to immediately go to your units and ready yourselves for immediate action, and that means now! All military and naval personnel, to your duties, fall out!"

Many of the assembled soldiers and sailors left, and some remained just talking to each other in what appeared to be a confused state. Edward yelled, *"I Have issued you all with your orders to immediately go to your units for immediate preparation to invade Wales. I fucking well mean now!"* He left to take his place at the head of his army, and all of his military and naval personnel did as he ordered. The ensuing military action defeated Llewellyn and resulted in him losing his territories just as Edward had predicted.

In 1282, Llewelyn's son, called Dafydd spoke to his people. He said, *"My people, I feel that it is time to rid Wales of the dominance of the bloody English! I want to do it now! I am now the Prince of Wales following the death of my father, Llewelyn. We will now join with other Welsh rulers in Deheubarth and North Powys to expel the English invaders!"* So began a national struggle by the people of Wales to rid themselves of the imposition of English laws upon them.

News of this was taken to Edward. He said, *"So the Welsh wish to try my patience! They shall learn not to trifle with me! I now announce that I am declaring a war upon Wales which shall be completely conquered, and it will become English Territory, the people will all be subject to English law, and they will do their duties and pay their taxes, or they will die!"*

At the next Orders Group, (conference between military leaders and their sub-ordinates) held by Edward, he addressed his followers. He said, *"Gentlemen, I shall personally lead the army against the Welsh, and the attack against those traitors shall be three-pronged. Roger Mortimer shall lead the attack column going into mid-Wales. I shall lead the column attacking the north of Wales, and the Earl of Gloucester shall advance with his substantial army in the south of Wales. We leave immediately, and all of you know where you are serving and what your duties are. To your duties, fall out!"* That resulted in the English army members all going to their assigned posts and taking up their duties as ordered.

Marching towards Llandeilo Fawr, Gloucester and his men were in for a difficult time from the Welsh who defeated them at the resulting battle at that place. When he was told of this, Edward was stunned. He said, *"So, the Welsh have beaten the army of Gloucester, that leaves me no option but to replace him immediately. Get William de Valence here quickly because he shall replace Gloucester!"*

William de Valance appeared before king Edward as ordered. Edward said, *"William, you now have command of what is left of Gloucester's forces. You shall be given replacements to cover those men who have fallen. You and your men are to raid in the south of Wales as far as at least Aberystwyth, closing with and killing the Welsh enemy where-ever you find them."* William replied, *"Yes, my liege, it shall be done as you desire!"* He then left to perform his duty. After a long time spent without sighting the enemy units,

William de Valance, the Earl of Pembroke arrived at Aberystwyth and reported that he had not even sighted the enemy.

On 6/November/1282, John Peckham, who was the Archbishop of Canterbury, was conducting peace negotiations. Meanwhile, Luke de Tany, who was Edward's commander at Anglesey, was holding an Orders group with his sub-ordinates. Luke said *"I want us to launch a surprise attack upon the Welsh positions which appear to be surrounded by water making our approaches rather difficult! So, let us hear some ideas of how we can successfully assault the Welsh and have minimal causalities ourselves!"*

For some time, there was silence. Then a knight stood up and began to speak. He said, *"Sir if we were to build a pontoon bridge between here and the mainland, we could easily engage the Welsh in battle and inflict a severe defeat upon them by using our infantry backed up by cavalry forces. Using the pontoon bridge, we could surprise the enemy and wipe them out!"*

The response pleased William. He said, *"Use a pontoon bridge to enable us to close with and kill the enemy! By doing so, we can use both cavalry and infantry units! May you be blessed by God and his mother, Sir Knight! What an excellent idea! See to it that the pontoon bridge is built immediately!"*

And so, the pontoon bridge was constructed, a fact not missed by the Welsh units in the area. The Welsh commander saw that Luke de Tany and his units were crossing the bridge and spoke to his men. He said,

"Men observe the English, they appear to be massing for a surprise attack against us. That can only mean that they intend to use the pontoon bridge that they are building to attempt to storm us. We will give them a false sense of security. We shall let them cross the bridge unhindered and let them get a lot closer to where our main encampment is.

As you know, the closer they get to our encampment, the heavier is the undergrowth. We will all hide along the path near the camp, and we shall ambush the English as they move into the camp area. You must not leave any alive!" And so, the Welsh successfully carried out their ambush of Luke de Tany and his men, causing heavy losses among the English at the Battle of Moelydon.

The forces of Llywelyn were noted to be marching out of North Wales towards Builth in mid-Wales. That intelligence was taken to King Edward I. He said, *"Very good messenger, you have done your work very well. Be sure to both eat and drink your fill at the Royal Kitchen before you resume your duties."* He then called out to his orderlies. He said, *"Orderlies and messengers take word to all commanders that we move to Orewin Bridge immediately to trap Llywelyn when he gets there!"* The messages were sent, and as a result, Llywelyn was killed on 11th of December 1282.

Edward raised a new army and marched into Snowdonia in January 1283, allowing him to take Dolwyddelan Castle which was located in the heartland of Welsh resistance. Meanwhile, de Valence was applying pressure from the south. The combination of assaults in the north and south was too much for the Welsh forces. In June of 1283, Dafydd who had succeeded his brother as the prince was captured.

As Dafydd was being led away, a guard said, *"Well, Taffy, I am glad that I am not in your shoes! King Edward is going to court-martial you for treason, and you can expect no mercy!"* As soon as the king had been informed of Dafydd's capture, the court-martial was set into place.

King Edward the First said, *"Dafydd the Prince of Wales, I find that you are guilty of treason and therefore, you shall die the death of a traitor! First, we will hang you, but not long enough to kill you. Then the torturers will stretch you on the rack and break your bones. After that, you will have your fingers and toes chopped off. You shall beg for death before it finally releases you from your pain!*

Finally, you shall be quartered, and your body parts will be buried in different locations in England and Wales such that no-one will ever know where your body parts are buried, and that will stop your followers from making a martyred hero of you! May God have mercy upon your soul because you will have none of it while you are here on earth!"

Edward was discussing the problem of rebellion in Wales with his sub-ordinates. He said, *"I need to you to come up with workable ideas of how to end the uprisings against English rule here in Wales"* There was silence in response. That prompted Edward to shout, *"What is it with you lot? Whenever I ask you for sound advice, it is usually not forthcoming, and I must usually deal with everything myself! Now stop your wailing and doing nothing, you always are just fucking around! I have asked you for a possible workable solution to the problem of uprisings and rebellions by the Welsh people! Now come up with some good suggestions or lose your positions and your lands!"*

A knight had been listening, and he now spoke. He said, *"My Liege, methinks that to control the Welsh people, you should give them a prince. You have beaten the Welsh, and you have executed one of their princes. I suggest that you now progressively incorporate the whole of Wales into the kingdom of England by firstly making many land grants to English barons who could then move into Wales with their armies and keep order among the Welsh by the building of many 'marcher castles' from which their armies could sally forth and impose your will upon the Welsh! Also, you should get more English people to permanently settle in Wales!*

To lessen the hostility of the Welsh towards us, I further suggest that you appoint your own son as the "Prince of Wales" and that this becomes the standard way for all male successors to the crown of England. That is, to become a king; a prince would normally be the 'Prince of Wales' first!

It is now the Year of Our Lord 1248, and you have your son who was recently born. Let me suggest, your majesty, that you hold a baronial meeting at Caernarfon Castle at which you could also have Welsh leaders. When you are ready to do so, you should have your son called Edward, bought out lying upon your shield. You should then say to all present, 'Behold the

Prince of Wales who shall also be King of England!' If you handle it like that, your majesty, you should find that the Welsh problem will be eliminated!" Edward Longshanks was overjoyed, and he exclaimed, *"By God and his Mother, what good reasoning! That is what we shall do!"*

Finance and Expulsion of the Jews

William the Conqueror bought with him Jews from Rouen. By 1280 the Jews had exploited England to the point where they were prosperous and widely hated, but they were still subject to any level of taxation the king chose. Their money-lending businesses produced much profit for the Jews and considerable hatred against them. It was not legal for Christians to take part in money lending.

In the Year of Our Lord 1275, Edward issued the Statute of the Jewry, which outlawed usury (money lending). He held an Orders Group with his court. He said, *"Ladies and Gentlemen, I have outlawed the money lending practices of the Jews by enacting 'The Statute of the Jewry' and some of you who may have debts to Jews will benefit from the new laws. It is now illegal for Jews to lend money, and they have all been encouraged to take up other professions."* Time passed, and a messenger from a grouping of sheriffs was ushered into the throne room where Edward was sitting.

He said, *"Your majesty, it is my unpleasant duty to inform you that your sheriffs are concerned about the fact that noted practice of Jews is to shave metal off the coins of the realm in what the Jews are calling 'clipping of coins'. The result of that is that the Jews are hoarding the gold and silver taken from the coins of your realm such that they are getting quite rich from so doing that while the value of the coins of this country is falling! The sheriffs feel that you must do something about this outrageous behaviour of the Jews!"*

Edward exploded into one of his customary rages. He shouted, *"What?!! You are saying that the fucking Jews are shaving the metal off my coins and lowering their value while they keep the shavings for later melting down and re-use in other things?"* He was answered, *"Yes, Your Majesty, that is correct!"* Edward thundered, *"So the fucking Jews are lowering the value of my money while they are lining their own pockets with the value of the shavings of my money! This is Treason! I want at least three-hundred Jews arrested and bought here for trial! When they are found to be guilty, all three-hundred of them are to be executed for the crime of treason!"*

In 1280, he ordered, *"All Jews must attend special sermons preached by Dominican Friars. I hope that this shall persuade the Jews to become Christians!"* That did not work. In the year 1290, Edward enacted the Edict of Expulsion, and all Jews were formally expelled from England. During the meantime, the property and money held by the Jews were taken from them. That generated revenues from the royal appropriation of Jewish loans and property. It resulted in Edward having enough capital to negotiate a substantial subsidy in the 1290 Parliament. Things stayed like that until 1656 when the Jews were allowed back into England by the Government of England.

Edward was in discussion with the Chancellor of the Exchequer. He said, *"Chancellor, methinks that Parliament has on too many occasions acted as a brake upon what I am trying to do for England. My ambition is to make England Great and to achieve that; I need much more money. The way Parliament is appropriating taxes and money at the moment is time-consuming and an impediment to the progress of my armies!*

I am going to give you my vision of a new 'Model Parliament' which make things far better for the collection of the necessary money that my government needs to run England and which in turn, shall be making the country a better and fairer place for our people including the commoners or the surfs if you want to call them that!

As you already know, I have throughout my reign always held Parliament regularly. During the Year of Our Lord 1295, I am putting forward a major change. From that time, the Parliament, which has the secular and ecclesiastical lords, shall also have two knights from each county as well as two representatives from each borough attending the Parliament. While the presentation of commoners in Parliament is nothing new, what shall be new is the authority by which the representatives attend.

Where previously, the commoners were expected to only give assent to decisions made the ruling lord and gentry, the common representatives shall have the full authority of their communities to give consent to decisions made in Parliament. This action will result in me having the full backing of the entire population of England to collect lay subsidies from the entire population. Lay subsidies are taxes collected at certain fractions of the value of all moveable property of all laymen." Edward 'Longshanks' collected nine of these taxes, whereas his father, Henry III, only had four of them. This format became the standard for later Parliaments, and historians call the assembly the 'Model Parliament'.

Prince Edward

At Caernarfon Castle in 1284, King Edward I, (Longshanks) spoke to the assembled crowd made up of Anglo-Norman nobility and the nobility of Wales. He said, *"Bring my son out upon my shield so that all can see him and swear allegiance to him! As of now, all future kings of England shall have the title of 'Prince of Wales' before they succeed the former king!"*

The soldiers did as Edward had asked, and the assembled nobles of England and Wales swore allegiance to the future king who was the first 'Prince of Wales' of Anglo-Norman England.

Piers Gaveston

Born in 1284, Piers Gaveston was introduced to King Edward "Longshanks". After serving "Longshanks" well, he was bought before the king. Longshanks said, *"As a reward for the service that you have provided to the Crown of England, I am on this day appointing you to be a member of the household of my son, Edward of Caernarvon. I feel that he could benefit from associating with you. I admire your martial skills and your conduct in the field. I am hoping that some of your qualities will rub off and be taken up by my son. I consider him to be too effeminate, and it will not do for this country to have a poofter as a ruler!"* Piers said, *"Thank you for this opportunity, your majesty!"*

Prince Edward was in conversation with the treasurer, Walter Langton. Walter said, *"My prince, kindly get it into your head that you cannot simply go around raising taxes whenever you want to do so. If taxes are to be imposed or raised, you must first obtain approval of the Parliament to do so. Any authority from Parliament shall be given to your father, King Edward I "Longshanks" and not you. He is the current ruling monarch and not you! You are only a prince!"* Prince Edward said, *"Oh, I see!"*

Piers noticed that Prince Edward looked troubled and said, *"Edward, my love, what ails you?"* The prince replied, *"My father and his treasurer are holding me back from what I can do! They are withholding the money of the realm from me!"*

Piers said, *"Edward, my love, do not worry. In a few days, it will be on the twenty-sixth of May in the Year of Our Lord 1306. That is the day when I shall be knighted, and so shall you be. When we are both knighted, we will both have more power. Methinks that is when we should confront your father and demand more power for you!"*

As he was growing up, Longshanks was becoming increasingly frustrated with what he thought were effeminate ways of his son. Returning from a hunt one day. King Edward I (Longshanks) walked into the bedroom of his son with the idea of taking him hunting with him in future hunts.

As he was walking into the bedroom, he saw his son was naked, and bent over while another man was having anal sex with him. Longshanks exploded into his customary anger. He shouted, *"Get away from my son, Piers Gaveston, you fucking arse loving poofter! Go on, get out of my sight before I tear you apart!"* After that, Prince Edward and Piers were more careful that their relationship remained their private affair.

After the pair of queer lovers were again caught making love, it resulted in Longshanks erupting into yet one of his rages. He shouted, *"Piers Gaveston, I appointed you to the household of my son with the idea being that it would straighten him out, instead of that, that there are many reports about you fucking him! I am sending you off to the campaign in Scotland! See to it that you serve England well because if you do not, you shall not be permitted to return!"*

Soon after Piers and the soldiers went to Scotland, Piers heard about a tournament which was being held near them. So it was that Piers, and twenty-one other knights deserted their duties in the Scottish campaign and attended a tournament. Learning about that, King Edward 'Longshanks' said, *"Guards, you are to arrest Piers Gaveston and the other twenty-one knights who deserted their posts. This arrest warrant is to be carried out immediately!"* The men were arrested, but they had the good fortune that Queen Margaret prevailed upon her husband King Edward, to pardon all of them.

Having been pardoned, Piers Gaveston returned, and the homosexual relationship between him and Prince Edward continued. King Edward the First saw what was continuing to happen and called both his son and Piers to confer about it. Longshanks said, *"You Piers Gaveston have dishonoured my family and me! You shall immediately leave England. If you dare to return to this country while I, King Edward the First, am alive, you shall be put to death! Now, leave my England and do not return, you arse fucking poofter, you, and the likes of you disgust me!"*

Longshanks was becoming more concerned about the effeminate nature of his son all of the time. He discussed the problem with his advisors. Walter Langdon said, *"Your Majesty, regarding the problem of your son being considered to be a queer man, I propose that you get him married to a woman who is not just of royal blood herself, but one who is exceedingly beautiful and also forceful in both her demure and outlook! Such a woman must be able to sway your son and make a man out of him!"*

King Edward "Longshanks" agreed, and contact was made with Isabella, daughter of Phillip, King of France. At the meeting between the Kings of England and France, King Philip IV of France said to Longshanks, *"Edward, I propose a marriage between my daughter and your son! We shall work out the details later on!"*

Isabella

During the night of the twenty-second of December 1295, Joan the Queen of France, Queen of Navarre, and Countess of Brie, Bigorre and Champagne was in labour. During her labour, she had experience various levels of pain associated with the coming birth. She was being attended to by the mid-wife named Matilda. As Joan's labour was entering it fourth hour. Matilda spoke to her in an effort to both take her mind off what was happening and to ease the pain caused by the birth.

Matilda said, *"How are things going with this birth, Joan? You are entering your fourth hour of labour and from my inspection of your birth canal, I know that the birth is imminent! I know that many women who are going through the giving birth process often have dreams or visions about their unborn children. Is that the case with you?"*

Joan replied, *"Thank you for asking Matilda. Yes, I am getting some dreams about this child. I do not know how to tell the difference between a dream or a vision. So, I treat dreams as if they are visions because they are all the same to me. In my dreams about this child, I see that this child is a daughter. Assuming that is the case, she shall be named as Isabella after her paternal grandmother.*

She has three older surviving brothers who are named as Louis, Philip, and Charles. Her younger brother called Robert will die in 1308 at age of eleven years. In my dreams about her, I saw that she shall become the queen of England after marrying the son of the fierce Edward the First who is known as 'Longshanks'."

Matilda the mid-wife said, *"Joan, the birth of this baby is about to happen. I can now see the top of the head of your child. Take some deep breaths and push that baby out of you! Considering that you already have other children, you should now find this birth to be an easy one! Now push it out!"*

Joan did as the mid-wife had told her, and the room was filled with the sound of an infant's crying. Matilda delivered the baby and cut the umbilical cord before she handed the child to Joan. She said, *"Joan, you have a fine and healthy baby girl, just like you have predicted. You have already told me that her name shall be Isabella and I shall enter that name upon her birthing record.*

Isabella was the only surviving daughter of King Phillip IV of France and Jeanne de Champagne, the Queen of Navarre. From that time, she showed that her will was a strong one. It is clear that Isabella could read from the number of books she had.

During negotiations for the Anglo-French truce regarding the duchy of Aquitaine in 1298, King Phillip of France was speaking to Edward I of England. Phillip said, *"Edward, your wife has died, and you are getting married to my sister, Marguerite. I propose that this will smooth the way for the renewal of the treaty of English presence and ownership of the duchy of Aquitaine. Also, I put it to you that your son by your previous marriage becomes betrothed to my daughter Isabella. I would dearly like to see such an arrangement take place as that shall cement both of our families into supporting roles for each other and make your ownership of the duchy much easier for many French people to take."*

Edward I of England replied, *"Thank you, Phillip for this suggestion and offer! Now let us discuss the betrothal of our children. In order to secure the marriage between Prince Edward and Princess Isabella, I feel that a dowry of eighteen thousand pounds should be paid! Assuming that is approved by you, both of our children should be formally betrothed to each other and marry in 1308!"* Phillip replied, *"Yes Edward, that is what shall happen."*

He went further, saying, *"Welcome to my family, Edward!"* As the news of the betrothal of Princess Isabella and Prince Edward of England spread around the court of the French King Phillip after the death of Edward I (Longshanks), many people attending court started to address Isabella as *"Madame Yzabel royne Dangleterre, (my Lady Isabella, Queen of England.)* (Warner, 2016)

Despite ongoing disputes over the duchy of Aquitaine, King Edward II and Isabella were married at the *'Our Lady of Boulogne'* Cathedral on the 25th of January 1308. Isabella was thirteen years old at the time.

Night of the Wedding

Isabella was wearing a red mantle with yellow. Under that, she was wearing a gown and tunic of blue and gold. Edward II was wearing a satin surcoat and cloak embroidered with jewels. They were wearing crowns which were glittering with precious stones. Due both of them having good looks and their wearing of these clothes, they looked magnificent!

The wedding between Princess Isabella of France and King Edward II of England was a grand happening which was attended by five kings and three queens. The lavish wedding was not consummated by King Edward II immediately, mainly because of the young age of Isabella (aged either twelve or thirteen at the time). So it was that King Edward II spent the wedding night in the bedroom of his homosexual lover called Piers Gaveston.

Feeling lonely and not understanding why her new husband was not with her, Isabella walked around some of the halls and rooms of the French palace where the guests were staying. As she was walking towards the north east corner of the palace, she heard the sound of male voices and that made her walk towards the voices. As she continued walking, she took care to not be seen by anyone, and she could see Piers Gaveston was holding her husband in his arms and speaking to him lovingly.

Piers was saying, *"My love, I do not like this woman you have married! Stay away from her! She is only thirteen years old, and it will not do for the king of England to fuck a girl who is so young. You know that only I can give you what you really want. What you want is to be fucked by me. You are a queer and that is the way it should be! So, I shall continue to have sex with you as usual. But I do not want you to ever be with your wife, Queen Isabella of England, and Princess of France! Stay away from the likes of her and only ever have sex with me!"* Edward II replied, *"Yes, Piers, I shall do what you are asking!"*

With that said, Piers began to fondle the penis and testes of Edward. He said, *"Take off your clothes and then bend over, my love. It is high time for you to again have my prick up your arse!"* Edward complied, and the sex act between the two men began. All of that was seen by Isabella, who was deeply shocked by what she had both seen and heard.

Isabella quietly left that area and returned to her own room in great distress. She was thinking, *"Oh great! I am such an attractive woman that even on my own wedding night, my husband prefers the company of men and opts to have sex with men rather than with me, his own wife! This is an intolerable state of affairs! I shall discuss this very unsatisfactory problem with Uncle Charles de Valois and Uncle Louis d' Evreux. Hopefully, they can prevail upon my husband to change his ways!"*

After informing her uncles of the problem, things went from bad to even worse, when Piers Gaveston was given much of the dowry in the form of precious stones and money that had been paid by the royal family of France to Edward I. Her uncles did try to interfere on her behalf, but to no avail. After the death of Edward I who was also known as Longshanks, his son, Edward II continued to prefer the company of males at most times and that also included having sex with them.

Isabella was furious that her husband openly preferred the attention of other males, in particular Piers Gaveston to whom Edward had made gifts of precious stones which had been part of the dowry from her father. Her uncles warned that they would not attend their coronation unless Piers Gaveston was gotten rid of. Edward's barons made the same threats. After they had been ignored for a long time, the baron's revolts became a reality.

Coronation of Edward II and Isabella

The coronation of King Edward II and Queen Isabella took place with great pomp and ceremony on the 25th of February 1308. King Edward II then ordered that Isabella be granted a generous income from the revenues of the county of Ponthieu in the north of France. That was his own inheritance from his mother. She was part Spanish and part French, her name being Eleanor of Castile – Ponthieu. When the French dowager queen Marguerite died in 1318, Isabella gained the ownership of the dead French Queen's lands. That enabled Isabella to promote her relatives called the Beaumonts and gain their favour with her husband, King Edward II. For his part, Edward turned the custody of the great seal over to Isabella several times.

Isabella and Edward Campaign Together

Isabella went on campaign with Edward in 1319 against Scotland. She was noticed by Scottish scouts who reported her presence with the English forces invading Scotland directly to their superior officers in

October of 1322. One of the scouts was known as Hamish Plenderlief.

He went towards the station of his superior and finally managed to both find and talk to him. Hamish said, *"Sir, I have just returned from a patrol which was conducted in the region around Tynemouth Priory. My second scout and myself observed that the English King Edward II has been joined in his illegal invasion of Scotland by his Queen, Isabella!*

His superior was Malcolm McGregor who was working with and fighting for Scottish independence on behalf of Robert de Bruce, who was soon to become the Scottish King.

As Hamish Plenderlief finished his report to Malcolm McGregor, the superior officer spoke. He said, *"Very well, so, the queen of the Sassenachs has come to our country in an effort to help her husband to hunt us down! I think that it would be most unlikely for her to share the camp of her husband's army because of the vile nature of Sassenach males. Therefore, I believe that she shall be in Tynemouth Priory and that is where we shall take her captive!"*

McGregor went on to say, *"Hamish, Take word of this situation directly to Robert de Bruce, who is currently in the Glasgow area. Let him know that Sassenach Queen Isabella is at Tynemouth Priory and that we are going to capture her! She will fetch us a pretty high ransom from the Sassenach King!"*

Hamish Plenderlief was a good soldier, and he quickly checked his equipment before he both ate and drank prior to mounting his horse. He was about to ride off when McGregor again spoke to him. McGregor said, *"Hamish, forget about going to Glasgow, news that just came in says that you may find Robert de Bruce at Byland. Apparently, he is due to be there by the 14th of October! Now quickly go to Byland and give de Bruce the message!"*

And so, Hamish Plenderlief rode towards Byland. As he was riding forwards, he was seen by English infantry units. These units had one hundred longbow archers with them. An archer saw Hamish and shot an arrow into his horse. That resulted in the capture of Hamish. Under torture, Hamish let it be known that Scottish soldiers were in the area around Tynemouth Priory and that Queen Isabella was there.

Queen Isabella and her companions consisted of three 'ladies in waiting', but no soldiers. Isabella and her companions had observed the Scottish soldiers which made Isabella say, *"My ladies, there are currently four of us. We are all women and none of us have yet even tried to lift a sword, let alone use a bow and arrows like archers do. We are now in the Tynemouth Priory, but we must get away from here, because the Scots are threateningly close by! There is a boat at the edge of the river below, and we shall use the boat to escape from here!"*

One of her 'ladies in waiting', was called Mary. She said, *"You majesty, what if there are rapids in the river? We could all down!"* Isabella replied, *"Mary, stop being such a scaredy-cat! We are going to escape from here by using the boat! You can stay here and* entertain the Scots when they get here if you want to! If you wish to come with me, I shall not tolerate more of your whining!"

Isabella now became very firm when she said, "Ladies, you shall now get into the boat. When we are all seated, we shall see what we have in the way of oars and other equipment." The women were fortunate in that they found that there were four oars on the boat. With each woman armed with an oar each, they set off along the river. It was just as well that the women got away to Scarborough, for the English lost the battle of Byland and Edward came close to being captured.

Up to that point, Isabella was treated well by Edward, and he was generous to her. Speaking to Isabella, Edward said, *"My darling wife, I King Edward II of England and the owner of vast estates in France, hereby make a gift to you, of the county of Ponthieu, France! I have ordered that shall include all of its revenues so that your income is supplemented! My darling wife!"*

Over time, Edward openly preferred the company of his male favourites. Then he began to blame her for the Anglo-French tensions over Aquitaine. She took it all in her stride, and she consistently supported Edward's relations with the French Crown and his own barons.

Confrontation at Leeds Castle

On the 13th of October 1321, Queen Isabella was acting as the regent for her husband Edward II when she and her entourage found themselves tired and hungry and needing shelter near Leeds Castle. As the party of women and their small escort of English soldiers was approaching Leeds Castle, A loud and stern male voice could be clearly heard. The alert sentry called out, *"Introduce yourselves, and state your business with the wife of the custodian of Leeds Castle!"*

The sergeant at arms of Isabella's escort spoke to the sentry. He said, *This is the official party of Queen Isabella of England who is on the King's business! Now open the gates or we shall assault the castle and that will result in your own trial for treason!"* The made the sentry confer with the custodian's wife. After speaking to her he said, *"My orders are to refuse entry to Queen Isabella and everyone connected to her!"*

Isabella was by now, wearing a sword, which she had learned to use, and she constantly practiced using it. She now spoke. She said in the loud and clear voice, *"Sentry, I am Queen Isabella the Queen of England! Now open these gates or my armed soldiers will attack!"*

Instead of opening the gates, the sentry shot a crossbow bolt at Isabella. She saw that coming and knocked the bolt down with her sword. She took command of the situation by yelling *"My soldiers of England, This castle is full of traitors and cowards! Storm the gates before you!"*

Meanwhile, the original sentry of Leeds Castle had been joined by eight other men at arms. They all brought their crossbows with them and fired at Isabella's men. Isabella's armed escort had meanwhile broken through the gates and three of the Leeds Castle defenders lay dead within the castle court yard. When the additional eight men joined the original sentry, all nine of them began shooting their crossbow bolts at the escort of Isabella.

That resulted in six of her escort lying dead in the area near the gates. At last, the wife of the custodian of Leeds Castle surrendered to Isabella, who was furious at the way she had been treated. Speaking to the custodian's wife, Isabella was informed that this had come about upon the orders of the king's new favourite called Hugh Le Despenser the Younger.

After she had been informed of that, she angrily said, *"That is despicable! I have just been informed that the new male favourite of my husband ordered this outrage against my person and those of my ladies in waiting and even my armed escort! That is treason and methinks that that this type of situation cannot and must not be tolerated!"*

Edward II Discusses Sexuality with Court

King Edward II was discussing the serious situation including his own sexuality with his advisors, many of whom were openly critical of Edward's homosexual tendencies.

He was told, *"Your majesty, the earls, and barons, are very concerned about the fact that you are pandering to that known and despised poofter, Piers Gaveston. It is well known that you do not touch your wife called Isabella and that you have not had any sexual relationship with her! If she becomes pregnant, then we will all know that you are not the father of her child, because, currently, you cannot bear to be intimate with women. You would much rather either fuck or else be fucked by a man!"*

We, the barons of England and Normandy demand that you become normal and end these queer affairs with Piers Gaveston, the Earl of Cornwall. If you do not do so, then my group of nobles and magnates shall hunt down the poofter lover of yours, and we will kill him. The Leaders of our group of barons are Thomas of Lancaster and Guy de Beauchamp, Earl of Warwick. You had best do what we ask, or you may face a revolt."

That upset King Edward II of England. He shouted, *"So, you are saying that your group of plotters is about to organise a revolution against me? I do not believe any of this! The earls of Warwick and Lancaster are only two men with small numbers of soldiers, while I command an entire army! I also have the Baron of York, called Baron de Clifford on my side, so I shall always win!"* In answer to that, he was told, *"No, you majesty, that is not correct! De Clifford, the Baron of York is one of the commanders of the army of Lancaster!"*

By now, things were getting emotive. King Edward II was again shouting. He shouted, *"There is no way that the likes of you can win! I suggest that you* and the other plotters now implore me for forgiveness because you have all made a serious mistake. If you and the plotters beg me to forgive you at the coming church service at Westminster Abbey and then swear total allegiance and obedience to me, I shall forgive your transgressions and pardon you. If you do not do so, you and all of your followers shall be declared to be outlaws and charged with treason!"

His advisors and members of his court said, "Your majesty, there is no point in your becoming angry with us, who are your supporters and the members of your court. Your opponents are outside of this castle, and you should heed what we, the members of your court are warning you of!"

Edward II replied, "In order to please you, the members of my court, I have on two prior occasions ordered the exile of Piers Gaveston. As well, I am again ordering the that Piers Gaveston goes into exile! Shall that please you at last?"

Edward's main advisor said, "My Lord, methinks that your banishment of Piers Gaveston for the third time is both timely and required. However, my Lord, please consider the fact that on two other occasions of banishment, Piers Gaveston simply returned and each time the homosexual affair between the two of you resumed on a more intense basis. As well, your wife has complained about your treatment of her directly to her uncles and her parents.

The French leaders are apparently so upset about your sexual affairs that France could even invade

England unless you put an end to you affairs with other men! Do you understand, your majesty?"

Edward and Gaveston Separate

Edward and Piers were sadly speaking to each other. Edward said, *"Piers my love, of necessity, we must separate. That is something that I do not want to happen, but our affair is common news even in France. I have been warned about the possibility of war with France unless we end our affair and you leave England immediately, never to return! I need you to make your way to Scarborough Castle, where you should be safe from our enemies until you can leave England. There are many among my nobles who want to see you dead. Therefore, please leave before they can organise themselves and kill you!"*

Piers Gaveston answered, *"Edward my love, it is with a great sorrow that I leave you here in the mist of enemies and traitors who have the unmitigated gall to pass judgements upon both of us. I am leaving here for Scarborough Castle as you have suggested at about mid-morning of the morrow. I am only doing this in order to safe-guard you, my love!"*

Unbeknownst to both Edward II and Piers Gaveston, everything they had said was overheard by Broderick, who was a servant of Thomas, the Earl of Lancaster. And so, Broderick hurried to his master with the news that Gaveston was leaving for Scarborough Castle by mid-morning of the following day. After he received the news, Lancaster was happy.

He said, *"I have been looking for an opportunity to kill the poofter companion of the king for a long time! Thank you, Broderick, now take this news to the Earl of Warwick for he is also against the poofter affairs between the King and Gaveston! We must do something about this bad state of affairs immediately!"*

After locating the Earl of Warwick, Broderick told him of the conversion between the king and his lover. The Earl of Warick said, *"So, Gaveston is leaving the Royal Castle for Scarborough Castle at about mid-morning. Good, we shall be waiting for him along the way, and he will never get to Scarborough!"*

Having said that, he summoned his soldiers and ordered that a company of them immediately make ready to march toward the Royal Castle and wait in ambush along the way to Scarborough. His orders were carried out and the armed unit was in an ambush position when Piers Gaveston came into view.

Warwick yelled, *"Surrender Piers Gaveston, you are under arrest!"* At first Gaveston resisted, and he was successful in killing four of Warwick's soldiers before he was overpowered. Having been subdued, he said, *"Guy de Beauchamp the Earl of Warwick, I, Piers Gaveston hereby surrender myself to you on the condition that I receive safe conduct to York, and you can imprison me there!"*

Warwick replied, *"Gaveston, have you taken leave of your senses? You are not in the position where you can make conditions or give anyone at all any orders! You are under arrest by me and the other barons, including Lancaster and de Clifford! If I was to take you to York, you would find a way of getting word to your poofter lover, King Edward II, so that shall not happen!*

Instead, you are leaving here, (Deddington in Oxfordshire) *and you shall be imprisoned at Warwick Castle. Once there, you shall be put on trial for your life before a panel of nobles. When you are found to be guilty, you shall be executed by two of my Welsh soldiers!"*

And so, the company of soldiers and their prisoner made their way to Warwick Castle. Arriving at Warwick Castle by late afternoon, Gaveston was imprisoned until the following morning when he was awakened and given water to drink prior to his trial for treason.

Trial of Piers Gaveston

While Piers Gaveston was in a dark dungeon of Warwick Castle, he firstly went into a state of despair. After some hours during which he tried to kill himself, he gradually began to accept his fate and he fully realised that his trial before some barons would be his last days on earth. At mid-morning, a guard unlocked his dungeon cell, and he was taken to the hall of the castle.

As he was escorted further into the hall, he could see that fifty men were present. He was taken to a chair and forced to sit down. He did not know what was happening until he saw Lancaster stand up. Having done so, Lancaster said, *"This is a court of your peers, Piers Gaveston! You are on trial for the crimes of* treason and perversion and sodomy which are crimes not only against the King, but also, they are crimes against God! Do you plead innocent or guilty to these awful and heinous charges?"

Piers Gaveston replied, "I am the favoured companion of King Edward II! My loyalty to my king has always been demonstrated by the fact I have served him with distinction against his enemies in Scotland and Wales as well as other places! I have never acted against my king, and I would never do that! There is no way that I can ever be disloyal to my king or harm him in any way! Therefore, your charges against me are just a pile of fabricated rubbish!"

Galveston's plea was immediately challenged by the Earl of Warwick. He jumped to his feet and yelled, "Piers Gaveston! You were observed to be having anal sex with King Edward the Second! You say that you love the King and that you would never do anything to harm him in any way! Yet here you are, charged with sodomy and having anal sex with the King! The fact is that you are a shirt lifting poofter and that by you having anal sex with the king, you are guilty of offences against both the King and God! That means you are guilty of treason against the King and God!"

The Earl of Lancaster now spoke. He said, "Piers Gaveston, do you have any more to say in your defence?" Piers answered with, "My king and lord, Edward II, is my life! I shall always be there for him, and I shall always do what is necessary to be done in order to further his progress and happiness. I am and always have been, the loyal supporter of the king and I *always will be. This trial that you people are conducting is illegal because you lot are conspiring against the King yourselves.*

Yet you have the unmitigated gall to charge me with treason. You are only saying that because you have already decided to kill me. This trial is but a means by you to try to put a legal standing upon what shall become my murder, but you will call it my legal execution! If anyone is guilty of treason, it is you and your supporters!"

That made the Earl of Warwick get to his feet again. He now yelled at Piers Gaveston. *"Gaveston, you shirt lifting poofter, a vote of your peers shall now be conducted to determine your guilt or innocence. Now shut up or be gaged while the vote is taken!"*

He then addressed the knights and barons present. He said, *"Gentlemen, behold, before you is the disgusting shirt lifting poofter called Piers Gaveston, who has managed to cast his evil influence over the king. No matter how Gaveston tries to portray it, his actions are contrary the requirements of God and the law, both of which say that anal sex between men is forbidden!*

As such, the activity of homosexuals is not just forbidden by God, it is an affront to every man and woman. In particular, the activities of poofters are considered to be offences against women and God! You have been given proof that Gaveston is guilty, and I now ask all of you to cast you votes about this man. Do you find him to be guilty or not guilty of treason, of sodomy and of sedition, or do you find that he is innocent of these charges?"

There was a hushed silence while the knights and barons attending discussed the proceedings among themselves. After two hours had passed, Warwick said, *"Well, gentlemen, what is your verdict? Is Piers Gaveston guilty or not guilty of treason and other crimes both the King and God?"*

The Earl of Lancaster loudly spoke. He said, *"Piers Gaveston, this court finds you guilty of treason, of sodomy and sedition as well as many other crimes against God! Piers Gaveston, You shall be taken to Blacklow Hill, which shall be your place of execution, and you shall be put to death by two of my Welsh soldiers! May God have mercy upon your soul!"*

Piers Gaveston shouted, *"All that I have ever been guilty of was having a great love for King Edward II! What all of you are doing is illegal. You are simply murdering me! Well, fuck all of you! May all of you encounter hard times and may all of you be cursed, may your children all become crippled shadows of themselves and may all of you be cursed by God for what you are all aware all of, yet you are all doing so willingly! Let God send a plague accompanied by a pox to infect all of your family members and may you all die in shame for what you are doing on this day!"*

Warwick yelled out, *"Guards, gag this man and take him to his place of execution at Blacklow Hill! See to it that you take this vile and disgusting shirt-lifting poofter to the top of the hill and then kill him there in any crude way that may take your fancy! The more you make him suffer, the better!"* So it was that the two Welsh guards crudely murdered Piers Gaveston.

King Edward II is Devastated

As evening was setting in, a rider was observed to be riding fast towards the Royal Castle at Windsor. He arrived at the castle's courtyard and demanded to be brought before the king. A sergeant of the Royal Palace Guard was miffed by that, and he said, *"You are demanding to see the king immediately! Common people do not have that right! You must tell me what it is that you wish to say to the king. After I have heard that, I will decide if it is important enough interrupt the king's day or not!"*

The rider was visibly upset by what had been said to him. He now responded with, *"Get it through your ugly and thick skull that I am Sir Winter of the army of the Earl of Warwick! You will immediately take me to confer with King Edward II or you shall lose your ugly head immediately! Now lead the way to the king or die, you thick blockhead!"*

The sergeant of the Royal Guard then reluctantly led Sir Winter to the king's chamber. Upon reaching there, the knight dismissed the sergeant of the guard and then he spoke to King Edward II. He said, *"Your majesty, I have grave news for your ears only!"* King Edward II loudly said, *"All members of court and all other people are to leave here immediately! Well, do not just stand there, you are all to go somewhere else now!"* That resulted in all people who were present leaving.

When he was satisfied that he was alone with the king, Sir Winters said, *"Your majesty, I have some awful and disturbing news for you! Your friend, Piers Gaveston, the Earl of Cornwall has been found murdered about midway between Scarborough and Warwick Castle. It appears to be that the crime that has been carried out by bandits or something similar!"*

Edward replied, *"Thank you for this news, Sir Winter! You have said that the death of Piers Gaveston appears to be the work of bandits, however, I suspect that the earls of Warwick and Lancaster are actually responsible for this crime! You have done well to bring me word of this tragic event. I find it to be devastating! I am going to declare two days of official mourning of the death of Piers Gaveston, the Earl of Cornwall. As well, I am having this investigated, for I cannot get rid of the feeling that the Earls of Lancaster and Warwick are behind this affront to me and to God!"*

Edward & Isabella Have Their First Child

On the 16th of February 1312, when Isabella was aged sixteen years, the couple were at their hunting retreat when Edward suddenly took Isabella into his arms and began to kiss her and pay her a lot of attention slowly and tenderly. She responded by kissing him and she took off his garments. She then took off all of her own clothing until she was naked. Much to her delight, she saw that Edward's penis had become erect and hard. She then took his penis into her hand and guided it into her vagina.

After a normal gestation period of nine months, Isabella was giving birth. On the 13th of November Isabella was in labour. Her mid-wife was called Cynthia was she was a twenty-eight-year-old woman. Cynthia said, *"Isabella, are you hoping to have a son or a daughter from this birth?* Isabella answered, *"Cinthia, I am hoping that the child shall be a son. The wonderful thing about it all is that Edward appears to have gotten over his previous love of sexual intercourse with men and he now appears to be normal in so much as he is now performing his duties as a man, and he is satisfying my needs and desires for sex.*

So much for what the rumour mill was saying about him being a queer man who cannot have sex with any woman! I am now aged sixteen years and I believe that Edward's past experience of having male lovers was only because I was aged thirteen when we were first married! I am now looking forward to having more children with him! He has been good to me, and he provides everything for me and pays for my entire household staff of up two hundred people!"

Cynthia said, *"How are things going for you with this birth?"* Isabella replied, *I feel no real pain, but I feel uncomfortable in so much that I am finding that this giving birth is akin to having to pass a motion when one is constipated, and nothing wants to move. So, I shall be glad when all of this is behind me!"*

Cynthia then examined Isabella's birth canal and said, *"Isabella, the birth of your chid is imminent! A few pushes and you should have the job done and your baby in your arms! Assuming that you have a son like you wish, what name or names shall you be calling him?"*

Isabella replied, *"Edward like his father. My son shall be Edward the Third!"* that was followed by more discomfort for Isabella, who now asked for some red wine to help to dull her senses until the birthing process was completed. After another half an hour had passed, Cynthia said, *"Very well, Isabella, now push and push some more until that baby is out of there."*

Isabella did so and there was the sound of an infant crying. Cynthia cut the umbilical cord and washed the baby before she handed over the child. She said, *"Isabella, here you go, you have a healthy son, just like you said you want. You have told me that you want to name him as Edward and that is what I shall write upon the birth register. Congratulations Isabella!"*

A Loving Open Marriage?

In 1316, Isabella was again pregnant, and she felt uncomfortable. She had found that it was more uncomfortable for her than usual when she had to travel. She now decided to discuss this problem with her husband, Edward II, and she hoped that perhaps a solution to her discomfort could be found through mutual discussion of the problem.

So, she said, *"Edward, I need to discuss my current pregnancy with you. I am carrying your second child and although I am strong enough, I am also feeling a lot of discomfort whenever I have to travel! There are often times when I have to travel in order to act as your regent. I am always happy to do that, but somehow, I need to have relief from the pain associated with travel!"*

King Edward II replied, *"My Dear Heart, I cannot bear to have you in pain or any other kind of discomfort! I am concerned that by you travelling by carriage to the various destinations which you must reach, will jolt you every time the wheels of the carriage hits a rut and holes in the road. Therefore, Dear Heart, I suggest that I buy a litter for the transport of you which is horse carried and a new team of horses to do that job. I think that the litter must be inlaid with luxurious cushions that will add to your comfort, my Dear Heart!"*

Isabella replied, *"Mon tresdoutz coer, (My very sweet heart) please do that and perhaps I shall be able to continue to perform official functions on your behalf!"* So it was that Edward obtained the litter and team of horses as well as the furnishings for the litter. He paid for everything himself, such was his love of Isabella. Things progressed in a normal way until the 15th of August 1316. On that day, Isabella found herself in labour again.

Again, her midwife in attendance was Cynthia, in whom Isabella had complete confidence. As the birth progressed, Cynthia asked, *"Isabella, how is this birth coming along for you? Are you in any pain or major discomfort?* Isabella replied, *"What little pain there is, I can easily deal with! It is just that giving birth seems to me to be a lot having to pass a motion when you are badly constipated! Cynthia, can you please pass me a large goblet of red wine? I think that I would like to 'Dull my senses while this is happening!'"

Cynthia replied, *"Very well, Isabella, here is your large goblet of red wine! Enjoy it and then you must get back to pushing and doing everything that you can to get this new baby out of you!* Cynthia then inspected Isabella's birth canal and announced, *"Isabella, I can see the top of your baby's head! A few more pushes by you should do the job! Now my dear, Push!"* Isabella did so, and soon after that, there was the sound of an infant crying. Cynthia washed the new-born boy after she had cut the umbilical cord. Cynthia now said, *"Isabella, I must now fill out the birthing register for this child. So, I now need to know what names you shall call him."* Isabella replied, *This is John, of Eltham, he is the earl of Cornwall!*

There were two more children born to Isabella. Both of them were daughters. They were Eleanor of Woodstock, who became the duchess of Guelders. She was born on the 18th of June 1318. On the 5th of July 1321, Isabella gave birth to *Joan of the Tower*, who was named as such because she was born in the Tower of London. She eventually became the Queen of Scotland. Isabella was wanting to visit her family in Paris. In order to do that without fuss, she arranged for her children to have babysitters and wet-nurses as required before she spoke to her husband, Edward II about it.

One day, Isabella spoke to her husband. She said, *"My very sweet heart, I feel the need to visit my father, the King of France. I also need you to accompany me during the visit. So, will you please do that for me, and we can leave for Paris together next Friday!"*

Edward replied, *"Certainly, my love, I shall be with you as it is the place where any good husband should always be with the woman he loves. So, yes, I shall be with you during your visit to Paris!"*

Arriving at the palace of Isabella's father in Paris, Isabella and Edward were escorted to their quarters by the servants of the French King. After they had placed their bags and other belongings where they both wanted them, they relaxed and had some wine. Isabella was feeling amorous, and she removed some of her clothing. She had taken off everything except her undergarments and she now went to Edward and reached into his cloths and began to fondle his penis.

She was gratified that his penis immediately began to stiffen and harden. She said, *"Edward my love, make love to me now because I very much want your penis in my vagina now!"* Edward responded and they made love. Both of them were naked and they slept that way for most of day. Suddenly realising the time was early afternoon, Edward woke Isabella saying, *"My Dear Heart, wake up, I believe that because we have both slept in, we have missed our appointment to confer with your father. I think that we had best get dressed and see him. We shall have to explain to him that we accidentally slept in and ask him to forgive us!"*

Isabella replied, *"Yes my Dear Heart, we must do what you have proposed so that we can continue to have good relations with my father!"*

A Fire in the Bedroom

Isabella having agreed that Edward's suggestion was a good one, the couple then went to see her father. Like many other fathers, Phillip of France was a push-over for his daughter. So, when the couple explained why they had missed their appointment with him earlier in the day, he immediately forgave them both.

That was followed by strategic discussions between the three people and that was followed with a banquet. At that feast, Edward and Isabella enjoyed themselves and again, had too much wine.

As soon as they returned to their bedroom, they undressed each other. Then both of them fondled each other's sexual organs and they again made love. After that, that again enjoyed drinking more wine and again they made love. They were both naked and sleeping in each other's arms, when Isabella's left hand knocked over a candelabra which had four burning candles on it. The flames of the candles quickly set fire to the furnishings of the bedroom. Awakening because of the smell of burning, Edward stood up and scooped up his wife and although they were both naked, he ran down the stairs with Isabella in his arms while loudly yelling, *"Fire! Fire! Get help to extinguish this fire!"*

Guards and servants quickly went to the aid of both Isabella and Edward. A butler called Louis Despenser set about getting clothes for the naked couple. After both of them had dressed, Isabella's father spoke to them.

He said, *"So my children, you have had a narrow escape from disaster! Pease be more careful when using things like candles or anything that burns. I am grateful that both of you have not died in the fire of your bedroom. Edward, I thank you for scooping up my daughter and saving her from the flames!"* Soon afterwards, Isabela and Edward returned to England, where the conspiracies of Lancaster, Warwick and their associates was building up to a rebellion.

The Battle of Boroughbridge 1322 A.D...

The most powerful noble in England during 1311 and for a decade after was Thomas of Lancaster. A Messenger approached King Edward II. Edward said, *"Yes, messenger, what is it that you have to tell me?"* The messenger said, *"Due to the obnoxious behaviour of your great friend, the queer Piers Gaveston, your barons headed by Thomas Lancaster have closed with and killed your homosexual friend!"*

Towards the end of 1321, King Edward II received a messenger. He said, *"I understand that you have some important news for me, messenger, what is it?"* The messenger replied, *"Your majesty, there is a rebellion against you in the Welsh marches led by the Mortimers!"*

Edward replied, *"So, the Mortimers are rebelling as I have expected them to. Very well then, I shall lead an army, and we will put an end to the rebellion!"* He took the lead, and soon the English army of the king was in conflict. The Mortimers surrendered, leaving Edward free to attack the northern lords who took action against him when it was too late.

Lancaster spoke to his confederates. He said, *Earl of Hereford, you are to besiege Tickhill Castle and take it for us while myself and my army take on King Edward II."* What he did not know is that Edward II and his forces were marching towards him. After some time, the two sides finally saw each other at Burton-on-Trent. A knight in Edward's army was holding an Orders Group with his men.

He said, *"Well, Gentlemen, before us is the enemy. Somehow, we must get past this river and close with the enemy and kill him! Do any of you have any ideas of how this can be quickly done?"* A Private soldier called John Smith answered. He said, *"Sir, where the river is a bit slower flowing, we could place our armour and weapons into some water-proof sheathing which we could make from tanned sheep or cow-ides and then use that to wrap up our armour and weapons in one or two-man lots.*

To provide flotation, we should place much foliage of trees or bushes into the bundle which must be secured by rope to stop it falling apart. As long as these flotation devices only contain the weapons and equipment for one or at the most two men, the packages should float. That will allow us to get across the river very quickly and we could easily surprise Lancaster by doing so, sir!" The knight was most impressed by his soldier and said, *"Private soldier Smith, I like your thinking, and that is what we shall do!*

Go on then, the rest of you, you heard him, place your equipment and weapons on an individual basis into sheaths made up of tanned animal hide. I think that it would be of benefit to use whatever we have in the way of lard or other fat to rub into the hides and try to make them as water-proof as possible. Remember to use foliage to bulk up your packaged equipment so that the foliage shall give buoyancy to the packages of weapons and equipment. When your equipment packages float, just hang on to them and guide them toward the opposite river bank." All of that was done, and soon, the vanguard of Edward's army had crossed the river and was attacking the army of Lancaster.

Lancaster saw the Royal Forces commanded by Sir Andrew de Harcla were coming at him and realised that he was badly outnumbered. He therefore retreated. Calling an Orders Group, Lancaster spoke. He said, *"Gentlemen, many of our castles have surrendered to the king. The re-inforcements which we were promised have evaporated, and I would like to hold out in Pontefract Castle if you still let me!"* His comrades said, *"Lancaster, we prefer to continue northwards!"* Lancaster let that be the decision, and the rebels continued northwards and reached Boroughbridge on Tuesday the 16th of March 1322.

Location of Boroughbridge Battlefield

The town of Boroughbridge is located where the historic Great North Road crosses the River Ure. Today, (2023) the bridge at the northern end of the town is the approximate position of the old bridge across which the rebel barons tried to force a passage. The hill to the north of the bridge was used for new housing estates as of 1993. It would have been the ideal place for de Harcla to deploy parts of his forces.

At an Orders Group held by the rebel barons, Lancaster said, *"Gentlemen, our tasks are simple, we must close with and kill the forces of Sir Andrew de Harcla and take the bridge which he and his forces are holding. Our scouts have reported to me that King Edward II is coming this way with a very large army and that means that we must quickly take the bridge or else get out of this area, or we are all doomed. If we cannot take the bridge, then we must make use of the ford across the river to get away from here. The ford can be found by our men a few hundred yards east of the bridge near Milby! To the south-east of Boroughbridge is the ancient Roman town of Isurium. The ford is the main means of crossing the Ure River for the townsfolk!"*

The Battle is Nigh

Sir Andrew de Harcla was famous as a knight, and he was also the sheriff of Carlisle. Fearing that the rebel barons intended to join forces with the Scots, he issued orders. He said, *"We must prevent the rebel barons from joining with Scottish units because if they manage to do so, it will go badly for the King and England!*

Messengers, you are to ride forth and using the authority, which is yours to act under the King's commission, you shall summon under very heavy penalties, the knights, esquires, and all other able men of the counties of Cumberland and Westmoreland. You are to compulsory acquire all men who can bear arms to assemble for the aid of the king against the forces of the Earl Lancaster!

We are now at Ripon. Here one of my spies has informed me that Lancaster and his rebel barons are going to arrive at Boroughbridge in the early morning! All Royal Army units shall immediately depart for Boroughbridge which is only four miles away from here. Messengers, when you bring the extra soldiers from Cumberland and Westmoreland, make sure that you bring them all to Boroughbridge where the King shall need them! When we arrive at Boroughbridge, we shall take the bridge itself as well as the town After that, we shall see to it that all of our men remain invisible to the enemy!"

The orders were carried out with the result that the bridge was occupied, as was the town. All horses were sent to the rear areas to ensure that the presence of the King's forces would give away the fact that the King's men were in place at the locations in and around Boroughbridge. All of the knights and some pikemen were on foot were at the northern end of the bridge.

Other pikemen were stationed in shiltron, opposite the ford to provide access to water and to prevent the cavalry forces of Lancaster from entering the conflict. De Harcla said, *"Archers, I need you all to keep up a constant discharge of arrows into the enemy as he approaches us. Your important task must be to inflict as great a toll of the enemy as is possible! Now get out there and give the bastards hell!"*

On Sunday the 16th of March 1322, the rebel earls and barons arrived in force and saw that the pikemen of Andrew de Harcla had occupied the northern end of the bridge. That resulted in the Earl of Hereford and Sir Rodger de Clifford, the baron of York conferring. Hereford spoke to de Clifford.

He said, *"Roger, we have some major problems in that enemy pikemen are occupying the bridge and the ford. Those enemies at the ford will be an obstacle to our cavalry when it arrives and tries to help us out in the fighting, so we must do something about both those enemies and the enemy soldiers who are here on this bridge!"*

Rodger de Clifford was not just a knight; he was known as an able warrior. He spoke to Lancaster. He said, *"Sir if we both charge forward as boldly as possible with our colours flying and with courage and aggressive hearts, we shall beat the weak as piss King's men!"*

Lancaster said, *"Very well, Roger! I have with us my standard-bearer, Sir Ralf de Applinsdene, and he shall be leading us when we attack the enemy before us!"*

That resulted in de Clifford, Applinsdene and some other knights and their soldiers rushing forward to engage the enemy in combat. The result of that action was that Lancaster went to join his cavalry forces while de Clifford and others closed with the enemy on the bridge. Rodger de Clifford and others were boldly rushing forth only to be wounded by arrows, spears, and pikes, resulting in their being driven back. Most of the men in this group suffered wounds, but they were able to escape for the time being.

Meanwhile, the Earl of Lancaster and his cavalry were approaching the ford during the early morning hours. Just as the centre of his column of mounted soldiers was crossing the ford, a voice yelled out very loudly, *"They are in the killing ground! Archers, aim and let loose your arrows from your longbows as well as the bolts from your crossbows!"* That resulted in clouds of arrows and bolts raining down upon Lancaster and his men.

Lancaster yelled out, *"Retreat, retreat to the bank of the river we just came from. Get out of here now, before we are all dead men!"* So complete was the disaster which had befallen his cavalry units that Lancaster sent a message to Sir Andrew. It said, *"Sir Andrew de Harcla, I, the Earl of Lancaster, hereby request an armistice until the morning. When that comes, I shall either engage you in battle or else I shall surrender to you. I await your answer!" Regards – Lancaster*

Andrew received the messenger and agreed to the proposal. After the messenger departed to take the news to Lancaster, he spoke. He said, *"I want all of my soldiers to have their wits about them at all times. All alcoholic drink is banned until this is over! Double the amount of men on guard, I do not trust the rebel barons and their minions!"*

Things were bad for the rebel forces. During that night, the Earl of Hereford's men deserted and fled. To make matters much worse, many of the men of the units of the Earl of Lancaster and Baron de Clifford also deserted them. In the morning, therefore, the Earl of Lancaster, Baron de Clifford, Lord de Mowbray, and all men who remained with them surrendered to Sir Andrew. He took them as prisoners to York, where they were confined in a castle to await, the pleasure of King Edward II.

The Trial of Baron Roger de Clifford

King Edward II had been notified in writing that the barons had been defeated and were now prisoners held at the keep of York Castle. He was notified by Sir Andrew de Harcla, who had written a message to him. The King said, *"Good, it is just as well that I have men such as de Harcla who can right the wrongs inflicted upon me by those who are supposed to be my loyal subjects, but who are not!" In the morning, we shall travel to York and stay at the Bailey Hill Castle! In the meantime, move Baron de Clifford from the Keep of York Castle to secure imprisonment within Bailey Hill Castle in York.*

I wish to give him and some other rebel barons a show trial during which I shall be the judge, and I shall have great pleasure in the sentencing of the Baron of York, Sir Roger de Clifford to be hanged in chains from the battlements of the keep of his own castle! Instead of confining him in the keep of York Castle, I want him to be confined at the keep of the Baile Hill Castle in York.

I want that to be the case so that when the time comes to hang him in public, he shall be placed onto a wagon which has a large "T" piece fixed to the centre of the wagon's tray. Bloody de Clifford shall be bound to the "T" piece, and he will not be able to move. That way, he will have to endure the rotten fruit and eggs thrown at him from the bystanders watching the progress of the execution wagon as it makes its way from the Baile Hill Castle to York Castle. All of the other traitors are to be held within the Keep of York Castle."

The Sentence

So it was that the prisoners were taken to York castle and imprisoned in its Keep. The trial of fifth Baron of York, Sir Roger de Clifford began and was very soon over. King Edward II said, *"Baron Sir Roger de Clifford, this court has found you to be guilty of treason in that you have taken up arms and sided with other rebels against your King! Everyone in this realm has had high expectations that you would be the backbone of the English aristocracy, but you have instead chosen to work and fight against your country and your King!*

As your King, I am amazed that a great warrior of your prowess could have taken military action against me, your King. Your position is that of the Baron of York, and you have been knighted. You showed what a great warrior you are during your past service to me, and for that, I thank you. However, it is treason that you have committed by siding with the rebels!

For that, the penalty is death by hanging in chains! I, King Edward II, now sentence you to be taken from this locality of your confinement at Baile Hill. On the twenty-third of March in the Year of Our Lord 1322, You shall be placed upon a criminal's 'Condemned' wagon, where you shall be bound to the "T" piece in the centre of it. Your hands and feet shall be bound to the "T" piece so that you cannot move, and you are kept you in a standing position for the entire journey, as the wagon travels towards the Keep of York Castle.

As you complete the journey to your place of execution, many people will throw rotten fruit, vegetables and eggs at you, a traitor, and that is what you deserve! When you arrive at the keep of your York Castle, and you will be taken up to battlements of the keep. When you have arrived there, a rope shall be fastened to your neck, with the other end of the rope attached to the battlements, and then then you shall be thrown off the battlements. May God have mercy on your soul, for you shall not have any mercy while you are alive!"

So, it happened that the fifth Baron of York, Sir Roger de Clifford was bound to "T" piece in the centre of the 'condemned' wagon. As the wagon proceeded towards York Castle, several inns were passed. As this was occurring, some people came forth with containers of ale for the condemned man, but the guards chased away these people.

They said, *"He cannot have any booze; he is on the wagon!"* Eventually, the procession reached the destination of York Castle. Sir Roger de Clifford was taken from the wagon and manhandled to the top of the keep of York Castle. When they arrived at the top, they found that King Edward II was there.

He said, *"De Clifford, it is only because of your past services to the crown that I do not order you to be flogged in such a way that it will peel most of the skin from your back, but still have you conscious and in great pain before your hanging takes place. You shall now have the rope fastened around your neck, while the other end of the twelve feet long rope is fastened to the battlements. You will not be given any reprieve or mercy. Do you have any last words before the sentence is carried out?"*

De Clifford answered, *"Fuck you, you useless arsehole and poofter, just get on with it!"* Next, de Clifford was pushed from the top of the keep, and his neck was broken when he reached the end of the rope. Sometime after the public hanging of Baron de Clifford, people began to call the keep of York Castle "Clifford's Tower."

Le Despenser Family

Hugh Le Despenser, Earl of Winchester was born in 1262, at Gloucester, England. He was also known as Hugh the Elder. In 1295, he was summoned to Parliament and became a baron. He distinguished himself by fighting in France and Scotland for the father of King Edward II who was Edward I, also known as *Longshanks*. After that, Edward the First sent him on several tours of duty as an ambassador for England, including two tours of duty as ambassador to the Pope.

He was one of the very few supporters of Piers Gaveston. After the death of Gaveston in 1312, he became the king's main advisor until Thomas, the Earl of Lancaster managed to have him dismissed from court during February of 1315.

So it was that Hugh Le Despenser the Elder stopped working at court for the king. He went on working and scheming to further the interests of his son who was also named as Hugh Le Despenser. In order to end the confusion caused by both of them having the same Christian name, the nick-name of *'the Elder'* was applied to him, and *'The Younger'* to his son.

After watching how his son was progressing and not liking what he saw, Hugh Le Despenser the Elder held an urgent heart to heart conference with his son known as Hugh Le Despenser the Younger. The first to speak was Hugh Le Despenser the Elder.

Speaking to his son, the Elder said, *"Hugh, my boy, I want you to go over to Eleanor de Clare, who is just over there, by the main feasting table. You are to introduce yourself to her and let her know that you find her extremely attractive and that you want to make her your wife! You must tell her that you are strongly attracted to her and that you want her more than anyone on earth! Be very sure that you make a great impression upon her! She is very rich and that will aid you to become more powerful in your own right!*

In order for that to happen, you must make sure that no-one ever knows that you actually prefer to have sex with other males! That must always be a well-kept secret and you must never let anyone know of your attraction to other men on a sexual basis. *Now then, let us look at how the Le Despencer fortune was initially set by me!*

Although most people do not realise it, Eleanor's Grandfather was King Edward I and he owes me two thousand gold marks! I shall consider that debt to be settled if you and Eleanor marry! So, go ahead and successfully woo her and then reap the benefits of being related by marriage directly to the Royal Family!"

On the 5th of May 1306, while attending the *'Feast of Swans'*, Hugh Le Despencer the Younger and Prince Edward were knighted. Being knighted at the same time and in the same place, resulted in the first contacts between Hugh Le Despencer and the Future King Edward II. The younger Le Despencer was being watched and guided by his father, Hugh Le Despencer the Elder.

The younger Hugh Le Despencer did marry Eleanor and the debt by King Edward the I to Hugh Despencer the Elder was settled. Eleanor's brother, Gilbert died in 1314,during the Battle of Bannockburn. That resulted in Eleanor inheriting part of the rich Gloucester earldom. Hugh Le Despenser through dishonest means, managed to get her properties transferred to himself over time.

Le Despencer the Younger Becomes King's Chamberlain

Hugh Le Despencer the Elder was again speaking to his son, the younger. He said, *"Hugh my* son, I have been watching your progress through life and I must admit that I find myself becoming concerned about the way you appear to be developing. I have noticed on many occasions now that you are quite effeminate and that worries me because when I am longer here, I cannot protect you as I always have done. So, in order to give you a life-time of protection, I believe that it could be best if you were to end up working within the household of King Edward II. He appears to be a normal man at the moment, but I recall the days when he refused to have sex with his wife, Queen Isabella!

That was something she resented because he was constantly enriching his male bedpartner of the time, called Piers Gaveston. The barons led by the Earl of Lancaster tracked him down and crudely killed him. Son, given that you are effeminate and that you lack many manly qualities, I think that the way for you to improve your lot in life is to become the King's Chamberlain.

If you are agreeable, I shall work towards that end, and we shall in due course have you installed into that position. When you have that position, we can see to it that we both receive many riches and lands that will give both of us immense power! So, please tell me, are you interested in becoming the chamberlain of the King?"

Hugh Le Despenser the younger jumped at the chance of easily obtaining a better life. He said, *"Yes, my father, if you could do that for me, it would be marvellous! I have heard many rumours which say that*

King Edward II is not only queer, but that he is an effeminate man himself! If there is even just a grain of truth in what I am hearing, then it should be possible that I become his bed partner and lover! Assuming that works out, it will give much power to you as well as to me! So, father, let us do that! When do you think we can be successful in obtaining our desires?" And so, Hugh Le Despenser the Elder began to implement his scheme of having his son appointed as chamberlain to the king.

Hugh Le Despenser the Elder said, *"My son, people have long memories for those who wrong them! I know that you have seized the Welsh lands of your wife's inheritance and that you have completely ignored the valid claims of your two brothers-in-law to those estates!*

It has also come to my attention that you have cheated your sister-in-law, Elizabeth de Clare out of properties at Gower and Usk. I have also been advised that you forced Alice de Lacy, the fourth countess of Lincoln to give you, her land! Beware from now on my son because people in high places are openly talking against you! I strongly advise you to always be on your guard and always be ready to leave England for other countries because if some of the people who speaking against you get their way, you shall be a dead man!"

Edward II Once Again is Queer

It is often said that *"A Leopard cannot change its spots!"* It is also known that if a man has latent homosexual tendencies, that they will in time lead to open homosexuality by the man concerned unless he has a very strong personality and a very strong will which can enable him to stop that from happening. With the Baron's Revolt successfully crushed and the leaders of it either imprisoned or hanged, King Edward II found that again, he was attracted to male companions, both sexually and platonically.

After several attempts by Hugh Le Despencer the Elder to introduce his son, Hugh Le Despenser the Younger to King Edward II, permission to do so was finally granted to Hugh Le Despenser the Elder. Upon being informed of that decision, Hugh Le Despenser the Elder was successful in having an audience with King Edwar II shortly before news had reached him of the death of Piers Gaveston.

Hugh Le Despenser the Elder said, *"Your majesty, I, and my family of the Le Despensers have always been there for you whenever you have really needed help! As you may recall, I have been the main reason that you are enjoying good relationships with the Pope and the King of France, because of my past service to your father, Edward I, who was also known as Edward Longshanks.*

It is the resolve of my son, Hugh Le Despenser the Younger, and me, Hugh Despenser the Elder, to continue serving you, our lord and king to the very best of our abilities for as long as we may live! Your majesty, in us you have loyal servants and soldiers. Since the defeat of your enemies at the Battle of Boroughbridge, my son, Hugh Le Despenser the Younger, has been working towards making your income independent of parliamentary committees.

I therefore urge you my lord and king, to consider making my son, Hugh Le Despenser the Younger, your chamberlain attendant! My lord, will you at least speak to him and then consider making him your chamberlain?"

King Edward II, answered, *"Yes, by all means, Hugh, see to it that Hugh Le Despenser the Younger arrives here at my court by mid-morning of the morrow! Everything you have told me makes perfect sense and that is the way things shall happen! I want to see your son in order to appraise his qualities!"* So, it was that at mid-morning of the next day, Hugh Le Despenser the Younger appeared in front of King Edward II.

As Hugh Le Despenser the younger was escorted to where the king was in attendance with his court, Edward II saw him and instantly was overcome with the desire to have anal sex with Hugh! Meanwhile, Hugh Le Despenser the Younger was going through the very same sort of sexual attraction towards the king.

Hugh went towards the king and prostrated himself at his feet. Edward raised him up and said, *"Hugh Le Despenser the Younger, your father has informed me of your qualities and how these can aid me. I am hereby offering you the post of being my chamberlain which means that you shall be at my beck and call at all times. Your duties shall be similar to those of a personal butler, but you shall also act as my intermediary between myself and the parliamentary committees in charge of raising money and taxations. These are awesome responsibilities, and I must know if you shall accept them or not. So will you accept the post of King's Chamberlain?"* Hugh Le Despenser the younger said, *"Yes your majesty, I do accept the post, when do I start directly working for you?"* The answer was, *"Now!"*

Hugh Le Despenser started working as the king's chamberlain and he was able to get the king an income which was independent from taxes and charges having to be approved by Parliament. Edward II was overjoyed by that and after dismissing the rest of court for the day, he called for his chamberlain to meet with him.

Edward said, *"Hugh, there is no point in us beating about the bush! I know that you are a queer and effeminate man. Also, I find you to be attractive, so, I want you to undress and then bend over, so that I can put my penis where it belongs, namely up your bum!"*

Isabella Hears and Sees Them

As she often did, Isabella was silently walking alone though the castle that was the home of herself and her entourage. As she got closer to the eastern corner, she distinctly heard what was said between the two men. She wanted a clearer idea of what was occurring, so, she entered a dark enclave from which she could observe what was happening.

She secreted herself from view and would have been invisible to others. She became curious as to what would happen next when she observed that Hugh Le Despenser was naked and now kneeling down in front of Edward. Hugh spoke to Edward. He said, *"Edward my love, I am about to do something special for you! Once you have experienced it, and when you want more of it, there are things that I must have if you are to get this sort of thing again!"*

Hugh Le Despenser then reached to the penis of Edward and proceeded to place his hard penis into his mouth. He then began to suck on Edward's penis. Edward was totally overcome by pleasure, and he exclaimed, *"That is so good Hugh! I can take that at all times!"*

That resulted in Hugh removing Edward's penis from his mouth and speaking. He said, *"Edward my love, if you like having me suck your dick, that is nothing compared with other things we can do and which you have never done! However, before either of us can proceed towards making your life an even more blissful experience, you must take both income and lands from your queen and give them to me!*

Let's face it, does Isabella let you fuck her bum? Does she suck you penis? Also, does she let you put your dick into her mouth and give you 'A Deep Throat fuck'? The answers to those questions is no! Only I can do those things for you. So, if you wish to continue with them, you must strip her of her lands and other belongings and give them all to me! Also, when the time is right for it to happen, I shall organise the removal of Isabella's children from her! I shall have them taken to a place where the children will be continuing their schooling and lessons in warfare and military tactics and engineering, but they will have no contact with Isabella at all!"

Edward was hesitant with his answer. He said, "Hugh, even though I do like having these homosexual moments with you, the fact is that I am both a married man and a king. As such, my first duty must always be to my country called England! Even though I have enjoyed what we have done, I confess that I love my wife, Isabella. Your demands that I strip her of her lands and other possessions, including her income and that I turn all of that over to you makes a mockery of the office of King of England and my position of being the husband of Isabella. Isabella is a good wife to me, and she applies herself with vigour to all assigned tasks that I set her!

Even though you demand that I take everything from her and give it all to you, that shall not happen. As well as loving her, I also honour her! I shall organise the granting of some lands and other things in such a way that I shall not have to take what is hers!"

Hugh Le Despenser the Younger said, "Very well then, Edward my love, I need you to take the children off Isabella and then see to it that she can never have anything to do with any of them! That way, I can get revenge upon her for you being at least partly hers! Only by doing that can our relationship fully succeed!

No matter how much you may love your queen, the fact is that there is a war brewing between you and her brother Charles, the King of France! I have declared her to be an alien person who is a danger to England! It has therefore become necessary to restrict her income and to remove her ownership of English lands! I have taken the step of confiscating her property from her!" He did not say that he transferred much of it to himself.

At last the sex acts between the men were over and they departed. Isabella, meanwhile, was still in her hiding place. She was thinking, *"So, Edward mon tresdoutz coer (my very sweet heart) you can act like a king and husband in the face of your queer lovers. Thank you, my love, for letting me see that there is an enemy working against me in my own home and castle. I shall now watch both Hugh Le Despenser the Elder and the Younger very closely for any signs of treason or other forms of aggression that both of them may use against me!*

Now that I know that both the Despensers are working against me, I shall be more watchful, and I will always remain on guard! Now we shall see if you, Edward can summon enough courage to stand firm against your queer male lovers and make sure that I am not bothered by the likes of Hugh Le Despenser wanting my income and lands!"

On the next morning Isabella spoke to Edward. She said, *"Edward, my love, I fully realise that part of you needs to associate with men only, and that even involves having sex with male partners. Be ultra-careful in your poofter dealings my love, because Adam Orleton, who is the Bishop of Winchester has been preaching from the pulpit in the church that you and Hugh Le Despenser the younger are practising sodomy and that is both a sin and a crime against God! So, be more careful my darling man, or you could find that the church will organise an armed rebellion against you!*

I also know that Hugh Le Despenser the Younger has ordered the abduction and keeping from me, of all of my children. That is intolerable and unless you stop it from proceeding, I shall rise in revolt against you!"

Edmund Fitzalan the 3rd Earl of Arundle Joins with the Le Despencers in Government of England

Edmund Fitzalan, the 2nd Earl of Arundle was born on the 1st of May 1285 at Marlborough Castle in Wiltshire. His father, Richard Fitzalan, had died in 1302 while Edmund was still a minor. For that reason, he was placed into the guardianship of John de Warenne, the Earl of Surrey.

During 1306, he was in the service of King Edward I and after serving with distinction in the Scottish Wars, he was richly rewarded, becoming the 2nd Earl of Arundle. After the death of Edward I, he became one of the many nobles who were opposed to both Edward II and his favourite of the time, Piers Gaveston.

By 1311, he had become one of the *Lords Ordainers* who assumed control of the government from Edward II. He therefore had a close working relationship with Thomas, the Earl of Lancaster. Being part of that, he was partly responsible for the murder of Piers Gaveston in 1312.

Meanwhile, his son had married the daughter of Hugh Le Despencer who was the current favourite of King Edward II. Due his actions in in aiding the king to suppress rebellions by Roger Mortimer and Thomas of Lancaster. Soon. He was within the inner circle of the Government of England by the regime of King Edward II and both of the Le Despencers.

During the time when Queen Isabella was in Paris negotiating with her Brother, King Charles IV of France for peace between England and France, a conference was taking place between Hugh Le Despencer the Younger and Edmund Fitzalan. Hugh Le Despencer the younger said, *"Edmund, we are getting many problems from Roger de Beler, who is the Baron of the Exchequer, and therefore controls all money in the land. We must be ridded of this brake upon what we can do, otherwise, the country will become a mess! Do you know of anyone who can rid us of the problems caused by Roger de Beler?"*

Edmund Fitzalan replied, *"I most certainly do! I have at times used the very efficient services of Eustace Folville and Roger la Zouch and the members of their gang whenever I have had to eliminate opposition to what I need to be done! I am sure that these men can also fix the problem posed by Roger de Beler and his activities at the Exchequer!"*

That made Hugh Le Despencer the Younger say, *"Excellent! Have Eustace Folville, Roger la Zouch, and their gang murder bloody Roger de Beler and that will rid us of yet another problem! In order for me to keep on having control of Queen Isabella, I still have the custody of her two daughters, and I shall continue to use them as weapons against Isabella who is a threat to my continued dominance of King Edward II.*

I have taken almost all of her land and titles from her, and I even convinced the King to reduce her allowances to the point where she had to dismiss her servants from her employment. As well, I have appropriated much of her lands into holdings for the both of us! It is only the Baron of the Exchequer Roger de Beler who is standing in our way! The sooner you can have him murdered the better!"

Things were put into motion, and the Baron of the Exchequer was murdered. The pair went on to misappropriate land and money as they saw fit, much to the annoyance of King Edward II and Isabella. Isabella was quickly building up her hatred of Edmund Fitzalan until it matched her hate for both of the Le Despencers. On the other hand, she continued to love her former husband, Edward II even though she was having an intense affair with Roger Mortimer.

The Bishop of Winchester Preaches Against both Le Despensers

The earls and others of the nobility of England were becoming alarmed that although they had removed Piers Gaveston as a threat to them, he was now replaced by anther threat which was even worse than Piers Gaveston ever turned out to be. At a meeting called to discuss the goings-on at court between themselves, It was suggested that that Bishop Adam Orleton address the meeting.

Bishop Orleton said, *"Gentlemen, you have informed me that the previous shirt lifting poofter and King's favourite called Piers Gaveston has been eliminated, only for England to face another set of threats from an even more devious and evil shirt lifting poofter who has been shown to have evil influences upon King Edward II. Gentlemen, you have proved to me that Hugh Le Despenser the Younger is in fact an agent of Satan!*

As of my next service at Winchester Cathedral, I shall openly and publicly ask God to remove both Hugh Le Despenser the Elder and the Younger from earth! It is because in both cases, they are out to enrich themselves at the expense of others! To make matters even worse, Hugh Le Despenser the Younger is guilty of sodomy, and he appears to have corrupted the mind of King Edward II! So, not only is Hugh Le Despenser guilty of sodomy, but he has also clearly corrupted the mind and soul of the King! That means that Le Despenser is in league with Satan and that he conspires with the devil in order to take the riches and property of the ruling classes of England! He must be stopped!

I have written to the Pope about this matter, because I feel that both Hugh Le Despenser the Elder and the Younger are guilty working against the country, against God and the King! We must now wait until such time as I either get approval from the Pope to help remove the King from power or we, the earls and barons start moves to replace the King and to end the lives of the Le Despensers".

On the following morning, Bishop Orleton was looking splendid in his Bishop's attire as he walked to the pulpit and began the Holy Mass service. He thundered, *"My friends and people of England, the country is in great peril because we could easily have the wrath of God upon us because of the activities of Hugh Le Despenser the Elder and his son, Hugh Le Despenser the Younger!*

The Elder is guilty of waylaying innocent people and taking their wealth, while the younger appears to be in league with Satan and he is openly practising sodomy Not only that, but he is a known pirate who has been guilty of many nefarious activities including the way-laying and piracy of the merchant vessels carrying legal cargoes for lawful English merchants!

It has also come to my attention that he has corrupted the feeble mind of King Edward II and turned him into his own homosexual slave! This cannot be allowed to continue! Express your disgust at the activities of the Le Despensers with everyone with whom you come into contact with! We must be rid of the Le Despensers and their evil ways!"

Roger's Escape from the Tower

In the year of 1322, Isabella was attending a meeting of junior lands department officials on behalf of Edward II, when she saw Sir Roger Mortimer walk past the shire offices where she was involved in making things work more smoothly for the crown of England. She liked what she saw and so, she asked her lady in waiting, named Eliza, *"Who was that man who has such a striking and handsome appearance?"* Eliza answered, *"My Lady, that was Sir Roger Mortimer!"* Isabella resolved to at least meet and introduce herself to the man.

As Isabella was interested in Roger Mortimer, she wanted to know more about him, she asked her ladies in waiting, *"Can anyone of you please tell me more about this Sir Roger Mortimer?"* She was answered by Katherine, who was another of her 'Ladies in waiting'.

Katherine said, *"Your majesty, I realise that things could be difficult regarding your relationship with your husband, King Edward II, but I caution you against becoming involved with Sir Roger Mortimer of Wigmore, because the Mortimers were involved in a rebellion against the crown before and during the Battle of Boroughbridge, after which Lancaster and de Clifford were hanged. I think that it is just a matter of time before the King orders the arrest of Sir Roger Mortimer and he shall be imprisoned at the Tower of London!"*

Isabella replied, *"That may be so, Katherine, but I wish to know more about him. Things such as what he has done, who his family actually is and how all of these things fit into the history of England and therefore, the crown of England!*

Katherine then told Isabella what she wanted to hear. She said, *"Isabella, Roger Mortimer is the descendant of Norman Knights who accompanied William the Conqueror. He inherited wealthy family estates and fortunes, mainly in Wales and Ireland He was the 8th Baron of Wigmore! Upon the death of his* father, in 1304, he became the 7*th* Baron of Wigmore. I know that he devoted his early years to obtaining effective control against the kinsmen and other relatives of his wife, who is a Lacy!

It is said that he established control over the Lacys who were able to summon Edward Bruce, the brother of King Robert de Bruce of Scotland, while he was fighting to become the King of Ireland. I know that in 1316, Mortimer was defeated at Kells and that is why he withdrew to England. After that, he was deeply involved in beating Bruce and forcing the Lacys out of Meath!

In 1317 he became associated with the Earl of Pembroke and his "Middle Party" in English politics; however, his distrust of both Hugh Le Despenser the Elder and the Younger drove Roger Mortimer and his uncle called Roger Mortimer of Chirk, make their submissions to King Edward II, who regards it as a form of treason! So, my Lady, please do not get involved with that man because I am certain that he will soon end up imprisoned in the Tower!"

Isabella answered, *"Katherine, it is now the 28th of November 1322 and what you have told me about him, makes me feel that he could be just the man I need to bring down the hated Despensers, both the Elder and the Younger! Both of those two men must be brought to justice and both of them must die!"* After that, things remained quiet until the 28th of February 1323.

On the day in 1323 at a Royal Ball held at what is now Windsor Castle, Isabella saw Sir Roger Mortimer and she decided to warn him of the peril that he was now facing. As others were dancing, Isabella moved toward Roger Mortimer until she was close enough to him for her to speak to him quietly and to not overheard by other people.

She said, *"Sir Roger Mortimer? I am Queen Isabella and I have some disturbing news for you, my friend!"* Roger Mortimer replied, *"Well, thank you, my lady, what is the news?"* Isabella said, *"Roger, I know for sure that you are on the wanted list of those who have been proven to have committed treason against King Edward II.*

I know that a warrant has been issued for you arrest and that a place of your imprisonment has been prepared for you at the Tower of London. I have a number of outstanding issues with the advisors to my husband called the Despensers! If you aid me in removing both Hugh Despenser the Elder and Hugh Despenser the Younger from court, I shall aid you in return!"

Sir Roger Mortimer said, *"Fear not my Lady, I shall aid you to remove the Despensers from their posts."* He had barely finished speaking when an armed party from the Tower of London arrived. It was commanded by John Smith. He yelled, *"Sir Roger Mortimer, you are under arrest!"* That resulted in Mortimer fighting the armed force from the tower before he was overcome. As he was being led away, Isabella called out, *"I shall visit you in the tower!"*

True to her word, Isabella arrived at the Tower and was escorted to where Roger was imprisoned. After the guard had departed, she said, *"Sir Roger Mortimer,* do you know why my husband, King Edward II has had you arrested and imprisoned here?"

Roger replied, "Most certainly Queen Isabella, Edward has had me arrested for treason. That is because I was part of the group to rise up against him due to his activity against my people! As well, there are many nobles such as myself, who in opposition to the king due to his queer affairs with shirt lifting poofters!

His affairs with Piers Gaveston were already bad enough, but now the King has placed Hugh Le Despenser the Younger into the position of King's chamberlain, due to the action of Hugh Le Despenser the Elder who was responsible for the Younger getting the position. He is using the position of King's chamberlain to further his own interests and England could be in trouble because soon of it!"

Isabella said, "Listen carefully Roger! This evening about mid-evening, I shall again visit you, but this time I shall have a man with me who resembles you! He shall be wearing a hooded cloak and he is very close to you size in both height and build. When we arrive here, you and he shall exchange clothing.

After that, with you wearing his clothes and with the hood of the cloak over your face, I shall tell the guard to release us. John Eckles, here, is my secret agent. He has already chiselled a hole into the wall near your cell. John, please show Sir Roger Mortimer the hole that you have prepared near the wall of his cell."

John Eckles now spoke to Roger Mortimer. He said, *"Roger, please come over here to this part of the wall where I am!"* Roger Mortimer did so, and John then said, *"Roger, please push gently against the wall here, at a height of two feet above the floor of your cell and tell me what you can feel."* Roger Mortimer did so, and he said, *"John, I can feel that the wall at that point is hollow and that the hollow section extends for another three feet in height and two feet in width. I do not know how you managed to hollow that section of the wall out, but it appears that you have done it!"*

John Eckles said, *"Roger, you are correct, in assuming that the hole is there for your escape. When Queen Isabella calls the guard to let her and you out of this cell, (he will think that he is letting me out with the queen.) you are to immediately go to the hole that has been covered with a thin layer of plaster. If you have to, enlarge the hole and when you get to the next corridor, use the rope ladder which is already in place, to take you to the roof of the tower. After that, I want you to again use the rope ladders which are already in place to climb down the tower wall to the landing where a boat is moored which you shall use to escape.*

Isabella again spoke to Roger, she said, *"Roger there in the boat, you shall find oars and you are then to use the boat and make good your escape from London. I want you to go to my Father's home in Paris, where you will be well received, and you must then wait there for my arrival."* All of those things were carried out, resulting in the escape from the Tower of London by Roger Mortimer.

1325 Isabella is Sent to Paris to Negotiate Peace

Edward II had his mind in turmoil while he pondered about how to keep both Isabella and his queer favourite on his side. He now gave Hugh Le Despenser direct orders. He said, *"Hugh, my love, you shall immediately return my children to their mother, my wife, Isabella! I do not care what you think about this, if you do not return the children to her, you shall immediately be arrested for treason and then you shall find yourself in the tower!"* The younger le Despencer said, *"I shall return her children to her, but the two daughter od hers are imprisoned by my father, and she shall have to deal with him to secure their release!"*

So, it was that Isabella was re-joined with her children, but not her daughters. On the first of March 1325, King Edward II suddenly said, *"Isabella, I need you to act in your role of Queen of England and my regent to go to Paris and negotiate with your brother a peace treaty between England and France!"*

Isabella replied, *"That sits well with me Edward my darling man. However, if you continue to have sexual activities with other men, that will upset me greatly! In the past I have had to always be in the background while you and your male lovers were having your queer ways! Well no more! I know that in the past, I have tolerated your needs to have other men as your lovers but that shall from now on be impossible!*

I thank you for going against your favourite called Hugh Le Despenser the Younger and returning my children to me. Besides Hugh taking my children from me, he has also committed other actions against me, including the taking away of my income and allowances which forced me to get rid of most of my staff! Unless you act against Hugh Le Despenser the Younger immediately, I shall have little option but to remain in Paris with my children when the negotiations for peace between England and France with my brother have concluded."

Edward said, "Why is it that you hate Hugh Le Despenser so much? You did not appear to mind Piers Gaveston when he was my favourite!" Isabella answered, "Edward these are the facts about your great homosexual love, Hugh Le Despenser the Younger. (1) He has always treated me, your queen, with disrespect! (2) He has stolen my jewels and even items from my dowry which was given to us both by my Father, the King of France! (3) he has gone out of his way to reduce my income (4) Last year, (1324), he confiscated my lands and that has left me in dire straits! (5) He got you to order the arrest of Sir Roger Mortimer in 1322. However Roger escaped from the tower and is now in continental Europe! Hugh le Despencer the Younger also took my children from me and for that, he has my special hate!

Edward my love, besides the crimes of Hugh Le Despenser against me, the Queen of England, look at his well-known other crimes! It is well known that he has seized the Welsh lands of the inheritance of his wife while totally ignoring the claims of his two brothers-in-law. He cheated his sister-in-law, Elizabeth de Clare out of Usk. He forced Alice de Lacy the 4th Countess of Lincoln to give up her lands to him.

He held in a prison cell, Llywelyn Bren holding him hostage in order to further extort him! During earlier times, Hugh Le Despenser the Younger also spent time as a pirate operating in the English channel. He became known as a **Sea Monster** *who was known to be lying in wait for shipping from merchants whom he wanted to extort whenever they used sea transport! Not only that, but his criminality also includes that he imprisoned Sir William Cockerell in the Tower of London and extorted much money from him!*

So, I have arranged for myself and my children to travel to Paris to see my brother and to arrange a peace treaty between France and England. Well, Edward, now that you know of the criminality of you poofter favourite, will you finally arrest him and execute him as he and his father deserve, or will you just let him get away with everything again? I suggest that you act quickly to arrest and imprison both Hugh Le Despenser the Elder and Hugh Le Despenser the Younger before you end up having yet another revolt of the barons!"

Edward was visibly shaken by what he had been told by Isabella. He was thinking, *"Hugh Le Despencer, my love, Isabella has informed me of your nefarious ways! I did not realise that you have been active as a pirate who terrorised the northern, north-eastern, and western sea shipping lanes around England!*

If there is even a grain of truth in what Isabella has told me about you past activities, then you have a lot to hide and that makes you both a thief and pirate as well as a murderer at best! I now know that you imprisoned various people and extorted their lands and money out of them!"

Edward decided to speak frankly to his favourite about these and other allegations. The resulting conversation between Edward and Hugh Le Despenser the Younger became heated and Edward was only stopped from killing him by the sudden, but temporary departure of Hugh Le Despenser the Younger, who left the palace immediately.

Isabella and Sir Roger Mortimer Meet in Paris

Roger Mortimer the 7th Baron of Wigmore was well received by the Royal Family of France. His reputation as a thorn in the side of the English King Edward II was well-known at the French palace. That resulted in Roger Mortimer living at the palace waiting for Queen Isabella to arrive, and the thought of his sister returning pleased King Charles of France.

Edward II of England had a letter drafted and sent to King Charles, informing him that Queen Isabella was about to leave England in order to confer with Charles and to attempt to resolve the issues which were currently bones of contention in the war between England and France. Charles was overheard saying, *"And so, my little sister at last, returns from that uncultured haven of thieves and rogues called England!*

I shall be most happy to see her, and I look forward to discussing with her, the many ways we can mutually support each other in our dealings with the poofter King of England!"

After many hours during which Isabella found herself becoming anxious due to her fear of the two Le Despensers having access to the guards of the Tower of London and how they could use the *'Beef Eaters'* against her, she and her children finally arrived at the French palace of her brother, King Charles of France. At the early time of 07:00 hours, just as the twilight was turning into daylight, the carriage conveying Isabella and her children came to a halt in the courtyard of the palace, King Charles appeared in person to greet his sister.

He said, *"Little sister, It is so good that you are here to try to get some sanity back into this awful mess caused by you husband, the English King! However, I am sure that by us sitting down and deeply discussing the mutual problems concerning both England and France, we can get into meaningful negotiations which shall benefit all of us! Also, Isabella, there is someone here whom I believe that you shall want to see. You already know this man, he is Sir Roger Mortimer, the 7th Baron and Lord of Wigmore, England! If you like, I shall have him bought to the drawing room used for visits by royal leaders of other countries at a time when it suits you!"*

Isabella thought over what she had been told by her elder brother. She said, *"Charles, please see to it that an escorted and arranged meeting between myself and Sir Roger Mortimer takes place in the drawing room that you mentioned by mid-afternoon today! It is possible that he could be part of the solution to the current problems in England which are being further extended by my husband. However, it is far more likely that the problems in England have and continue to be made to happen by both Hugh Le Despenser the Elder and his son, Hugh Le Despenser the Younger! Both of these men present real and continuing problems for England, and I must find a way of ending their evil ways and influence!"*

Charles replied, *"Very well little sister, consider your meeting with Sir Roger Mortimer to be arranged for the middle of the afternoon today!"* Isabella busied herself with getting some rest and preparing for her visit by Sir Roger Mortimer, whom she was thinking could aid her to put things right in England. Finally, with the time approaching 15:00 hours or 3 pm, a butler came to King Charles and spoke to him.

He said, *"Your Majesty, Queen Isabella of England and Princess of France, Sir Roger Mortimer, the 7th Baron of Wigmore is waiting for you to attend to him in the drawing room, as arranged by you!"* The French king replied, *"Good, butler, thank you for informing me, now take my sister Isabella to him!"*.

As she was entering the drawing room, she could see Roger Mortimer. He exclaimed, *"My Lady Isabella! How wonderful to finally see you again!"* Isabella replied, *"Sir Roger Mortimer, it is good to see you again and that you have escaped the Tower of London! Mainly due to the two evil Le Despensers,* things in England have gone from bad to much worse and we must not let that downward slide of the entire country continue!

I am conversant with you fine military record in support of my husband King Edward II, and I believe that you and only you can aid me in setting things right in England and then help me ruling as regent on behalf of my son Prince Edward. A problem with all of this is that my husband, Edward II is totally besotted with Hugh Le Despenser the Younger, who, along with his father Hugh Le Despenser the Elder is systematically robbing the English people of the riches and income of the country. They use the wealth to bestow even more riches, lands, and titles upon themselves!

When viewed along with their other past activities, it is very clear that both of these men are guilty of High Treason! I want you to help me to raise an invasion force that I can use to invade England and install my son Edward on the throne even though he is only aged twelve years at the moment. However, he shall be thirteen years old, next Thursday!"

Roger Mortimer said, *"My Queen and Lady, I, Sir Roger Mortimer, the 7th baron of Wigmore, hereby pledge my total alliance and service to Queen Isabella of England, who is also the Princess of France! With your permission, my Lady, may I suggest that we set about raising a mercenary army made up of Germanic and French soldiers to enable us to successfully invade England?"*

Preparing for the Invasion

Isabella agreed with that proposal and the arrangements to begin raising a mercenary army were initiated. Things were shaping up nicely for both Sir Roger Mortimer and Queen Isabella when Roger said, *"Your Majesty, we have been able to obtain the services five hundred French cavalrymen and nine hundred infantry soldiers! Most of the cavalry are Norman, while most of the infantry are Germanic. Now that we have these mercenary soldiers, it is necessary for us both to continually be seen by all of them and in order for us to be able to have their loyalty, we must not only pay them all on time, but we must also be seen to train with them and share their hardships with them.*

By us being seen to share both the hardships and the successes with them, they will bond with us, and we shall become victorious against both Edward II and both the Le Despencers! We must now make sure that we plan the coming invasion of England, and that we leave nothing to chance. I have already ordered thorough investigations of probable landing sites which we will use for the invasion.

The reports about these sites shall include the topography of those areas, including what obstacles we may encounter as well as things we can use such as forests, their locations, towns and villages and their locations from swamps, high ground, coastline, and roads that could be within the proposed landing areas."

Isabella was impressed by all of that, and she decided to reward her friend. In order to do so, she loosened her bodice, and her large left breast became fully exposed. She said, *"Roger, look at me, do you like what you can see?"* Roger replied, *"I most certainly do, my Queen!"* and he then went to her. They made love.

Edward II Asks Isabella to Return to London

As we have already covered, Isabella was sent to Paris to negotiate a peace treaty with her brother, Charles. Now that Isabella had most of her children with her again, she was feeling much more secure. She has again met with Sir Roger Mortimer, resulting in preparations being made for the invasion of England. During the meantime, her husband, King Edward II, wrote letters to her imploring her to return to London. After a period of six months had passed, Isabella again refused to return.

Instead, she wrote directly to her husband. Her letter stated, *"Mon tresdoutz coer, (my very sweet heart) I do wish to return to my home in London and to be with you again my love! However, within your court are the evil Hugh Le Despenser the Elder end his son the more evil Hugh Le Despencer the Younger. It is the criminal behaviour of both the Despencers that have made me stay in Paris, where I cannot be bothered by the likes of the Despensers and have most of my children safely with me.*

Remember that it was your queer lover, Hugh Le Despencer the Younger who took away my children and kept them from me for a very long time! When that is coupled with his other crimes of having been a pirate, of giving false witness in order to take the property of others and how he reduced my income to poverty levels while increasing his receipts of

England's revenue taking the property of others, I must insist that you immediately end your relationship with him as a condition of my return! Unless you immediately end your relationship with Hugh Le Despenser the Younger, I shall have little choice but to stay away from England!"

Having read that, King Edward II wrote a letter to his wife, Isabella. It said, *"Isabella, the love of my life, as you know, I deeply love you but there is a part of me that must have continual relationships and sexual contact with other men! Therefore, I must reject what you are asking for as being too extreme!*

Hugh Le Despencer shall therefore remain as my chamberlain and servant. I have been informed by others that you are in contact with the traitor called Sir Roger Mortimer! I remind you that is in itself treason and I urge you to stop that liaison with him and other traitors! It has come to my attention that you and Sir Roger Mortimer are in the process of building up a sizeable army and I therefore fear the worst! Return to London my love, before all is lost! Your Loving Husband – Edward"

Reading the letter gave some joy to Isabella, but she resolved not to return to England until she could invade the country with her army and install, her thirteen-year-old son as King Edward III. That would give her and Roger Mortimer the opportunity to rule as regents until Edward III was old enough to rule in his own right.

Isabella spoke to her brother, Charles, the King of France. She said, *"Charles, I want peace between your kingdom of France and my kingdom of England. Due to the fact that I am from the very same family as yourself, I cannot relinquish my property in France which is mine by birthright! I do, however, realise that my lands are part of France and that they must be subject to French laws and taxes. I shall work with you towards us both having a fairer land ownership and we shall negotiate about all other issues as they may arise!"*

That impressed Charles and he replied, *"Thank you, Isabella, my baby sister! I always thought that if I managed to speak to you, that sanity between our countries of England and France would prevail and we can live in peace! Your friend called Sir Roger Mortimer has told me of the disgusting life that you have been forced to live in England. I know about what has been done by both Hugh Le Despenser the Elder and Hugh Le Despenser the Younger!*

I have ordered that the current war between England and France is ended. That means that your mission to end the war has been completely successful! However, all of that is dependent upon your son Edward swearing allegiance to me in public. In order to help you raise a mercenary army, I suggest that you approach your cousin, Joan the countess of Hainault to raise a mercenary army for you consisting of a mixture of Franch and Germanic soldiers.

Also, France shall assist you and Roger Mortimer with invading England by giving you access to the necessary shipping required for your forces and

France shall also provide training and weapons for your army!

Also, Isabella, it has been brought to my knowledge that your country of England is either already in rebellion or else it is about to be in revolution because of the attitudes of the barons towards your husband, King Edward II! It appears that there are two sides in the civil war. They are the royalists who support Edward and those who want him removed. Those who want him removed include the Bishop of Westminster who by name is Bishop Adam Orleton. So, in other words, even the church is against the activities of both Hugh Le Despenser the Elder and his son, Hugh Le Despenser the Younger!

So, Isabella, all that now needs to be done is to have your son and heir to the English throne come here and pledge total allegiance to me as far as his ownership of Aquitaine is concerned. That also means that he shall become both the Duke of Aquitaine and the Count of Ponthieu. So, in order to get the Le Despensers to send you son here, let it be known that he must attend here and publicly swear allegiance to me over his holdings in Aquitaine, otherwise, the war between England and France shall continue."

So, it was with great joy that Isabella wrote to Edward. Her letter said, *"Mon Cheri, I have been successful in ending the war with France! King Charles IV of France has ordered that hostilities between England and France shall cease upon our son, Edward, appearing at the French palace and in public swearing allegiance to King Charles IV in all matters to do with*

Aquitaine. So, send my son Edward here immediately and overrule the Le Despensers!"

That resulted in her son, Edward arriving in Paris, and thus, Isabella was re-united with her son. Soon after that Prince Edward did swear allegiance to King Charles of France in all matters concerning English ownership of the French area known as Aquitaine and the current war between England and France was over. By these actions, Prince Edward now became the Duke of Aquitaine and the Count of Ponthieu as well as being in line for the English throne and therefore having the title of *'Prince of Wales'*.

Meanwhile, Isabella, her lover called Roger Mortimer and her other conspirators were discussing the coming invasion of England by them. At the meeting called to discuss the future invasion of England, Roger Mortimer spoke. He said, *My Lady and Queen Isabella of England and the Princess of France, we must now discuss getting ready for our invasion of England. In order to be successful in this, we must have people in England who know when and where we shall land our forces and when we intend to do so!*

During my service to King Edward II of England, I became familiar with the coastal areas near Harwich which I believe to be most suitable for us to launch a sea-borne Landing.

It is also necessary for us to have supporters in England who can pave the way for our coming by getting the people between Harwich, Cambridge, London, and Bristol to support our invasion by disrupting things in England. So it shall be very much to our advantage for churchmen and their leaders in all of those places to preach sermons about the evils being practised by the Le Despensers and how many much higher taxes must inevitably imposed upon the English population in order to counter what the Elder and the Younger Le Despensers want done!

In order for that to be easily achieved, our scribes must immediately make contact with the Bishop of Westminster, Adam Orleton. The last time that I spoke to him, he told me that that he wants to preach against the 'Unholy trio of Hugh le Despenser the Elder, Hugh Le Despenser the younger and the weak poofter King Edward II'. Scribes, draft letters directly to the Bishop of Winchester informing him that we are coming and that I want him to begin undermining King Edward immediately and also inform the nobles of Lincoln and Hereford so that they can collect local levies in our support.

I also want Thomas, the Earl of Norfolk, Henry the Earl of Leicester, and Thomas the brother of the Earl of Lancaster, who was hanged by King Edward II, informed that we are on the way and that we shall be landing near Harwich! So, scribes, you have an important task! Do not fail me or Isabella, because if you do, you shall die!"

Bishop Orleton Preaches Against the King

As soon as he read the letter from Roger Mortimer and Isabella, Bishop Adam Orleton who was the bishop of Winchester, began to plan and to write out his first sermon against King Edward as well as Hugh Le Despenser the Elder and the Younger. After many hours spent in writing and rewriting the sermon, he was finally happy with it.

It read, *"Members of the Christian Faith! Let us give thanks to God and implore him to remove the weak King Edward II! God must remove him from that position because he has consistently defied God by practising sodomy with the evil Hugh Le Despenser the Younger who must be removed from his position in the Royal Court. He is following the instructions of taking part in the heathern pastime of practising sodomy with the king and also committing the sin of corrupting the weak mind of the king from his father, known as Hugh Le Despenser the Elder!*

In both cases of the Le Despensers, they are committing their activities in order to obtain vast amounts of land, money, and other wealth to which they are not entitled! Pray to God in heaven to help us remove the king and both the evil Le Despensers from all official duties in the Government of England!

Due to the criminal activities of both Hugh Le Despenser the Elder and Hugh Le Despenser the Younger, God is very upset and even outraged by the sodomy practised with King Edward by Hugh Le Despencer the Younger, on the instructions of his own father, Hugh Le Despencer the Elder! The riots that you see taking place around you are a sign of the displeasure of God about how England is being run and by those who are not running this country according to the wishes of God!

My people, do something for yourselves and pray to God for the successful removal of King Edward

II from government and for the arrest and trials for High Treason by both Hugh Le Despencer the Elder and his son called Hugh Le Despencer the Younger! It is only the removal of those three men from the government of England that you can again enjoy the full blessings from God!"

The bishop read and reread the sermon, and he was finally happy with the way it sounded! He resolved to begin using it against the king and both of the Le Despensers as of the following morning. This was about to inflame an already serious situation, which was illustrated by protests and riots taking place in London and other major cities.

Meanwhile, Isabella ordered her scribes to write letters to bishops in Lincoln and Hereford. The bishop of Westminster, Adam Orleton, had been active in preparing for Isabella's invasion of England. Knowing that the invasion was planned to take place on the 24th of September 1326. Knowing that Isabella's army would land at Harwich on that day, he organised the preaching of sermons against the Le Despensers and King Edward II to congregations between Harwich and London.

So it was that Adam Orleton, the Bishop of Winchester was preaching at Westminster Cathedral at mid-afternoon of the 22nd of September 1326. From the elevated pulpit he thundered, *"My fellow Englishmen and women, our country of England is in great peril! I have seen a direct vision from God! He has told me that due to the evil Hugh Le Despenser the Elder conspiring to have his son, Hugh Le Despenser appointed as the chamberlain of the king and then both the Elder and his son, the Younger, are systematically robbing the Royal Treasury of money which they have used to vastly enrich themselves.*

The country of England has little money left for proper and legal purposes for such things as schooling the population and he maintenance of roads and bridges! Instead the money in the treasury has been used to buy vast estates for the two Le Despenser men!

Even more disturbing is the wrath of God because he is rightly upset because of the sodomy that is even now being practised between both the King and his chamberlain known as Hugh Le Despenser the Younger!

The fact that Hugh Le Despenser the Younger is a shirt lifting poofter is well-known to his own father, Hugh Le Despenser the Elder. He knew that his son would actively enter into a sodomising relationship with King Edward II, and he actively encouraged that in order to have the King's ear and both the money and power that would flow to him from being in such a powerful position within the inner circle of the King's Court. My people, God has commanded that you break away from King Edward II and both of the Le Despensers immediately!

To help England to achieve the will of God, he is sending us an army of liberation which is commanded by our own Queen Isabella and her lieutenants of Sir Roger Mortimer, Edmund of Kent, Jean d' Hainault and several other English noblemen shall be here to liberate us all from the administration of both of the le Despensers and King Edward II! My people! I can see no other way of saving England, so please join with me in getting rid of the evil in our mist and obeying the will of God!

So, my people of England, rise up and help Queen Isabella remove her husband, Edward II from power and instead, install her son, Prince Edward as King Edward III. God will bless you for removing his father King Edward II installing Edward III as the King! Please speak to as many people as you can about this, for England must force King Edward II to abdicate in favour of his son, who shall become known as King Edward III! Thus, England shall again have the blessing of God!"

That proved to be so effective, that most people between Harwich and Cambridge were in total opposition to King Edward II and both the Le Despensers, something that would aid Isabella's invasion enormously!

Meanwhile, the work of sedition against the government of Edward II and his regime of the two Hugh Le Despensers was doing its work! English people were openly discussing King Edward II and his two Hugh Le Despenser advisors, and they were confident that government of the royalists could not win.

Many people were saying, *"I just returned from a church Service at the Westminster Cathedral, and I am appalled at what the Bishop was saying to the congregation about King Edward II and his two close advisors of Hugh Le Despenser the Elder and the*

Younger! It appears that we, the common people of England must do without many things and even come close to starving just so that King Edward II and his advisors can live in luxury while they misgovern England and reduce the country to poverty!

Bishop Orleton said that England has help on the way from Queen Isabella who will soon invade England and remove the King in favour of his son, Prince Edward. It will only be after the removal of the current king that things can go back to normal, and England again has the blessing of God!"

During the early afternoon of the 29th of November 1325, a messenger was escorted into the throne room to give a message to King Edward II and his advisors of the two Le Despencers. The messenger said, *"Your majesty, rebellion has broken out against your government and that of the Le Despencers! The whole countryside from Harwick to Cambridge and even here in London is very close to open rebellion! My lord and king, you must get away from London and be sure that the despised members of your government cabinet go with you to safety! I strongly suggest that you flee to Wales or some other locality near there where you and the two Le Despencers can live in safety!*

Both of the Le Despencers are the sworn enemies of Queen Isabella who has declared both the Elder and the Younger Le Despencers to be outlaws! They shall be hunted down and put to death for High Treason and acting in a manner to cause affront to God in that the Elder systematically installed the Younger into positions of high authority! As you know my lord, the penalty, for High Treason is death by hanging as well as the charges of causing affront to God by the practice of sodomy shall result in the younger also having his penis cut off and thrown upon a fire while he is tied to a ladder at a height of 14 feet.

He shall also have his testes removed by being castrated in public and his balls shall then be thrown upon the same fire. He shall be disembowelled, and his intestines shall also be thrown into the fire! After that, his body shall be cut into four pieces and taken to distant parts of England and Wales and buried at the different locations in order to stop any possible action which could result in him becoming a martyr! Therefore, my king, if you wish to survive and if you also want the Le Despencers to both survive, then you must all flee!"

1326 Isabella & Mortimer Invade England

During 1325, an intense affair between Roger Mortimer and Queen Isabella started and quickly blossomed. As time went on, the affair between the lovers intensified. The affair between them started because Isabella was re-introduced to Roger Mortimer by her cousin, Joan, the Countess of Hainault.

Isabella had met with her cousin Joan because she was seeing Joan's husband, William, the Count of Hainault in order to obtain his help in raising a mercenary army for her. Joan, meanwhile, was busy trying to arrange a union between Isabella's son, Edward, and Count William I's daughter, called Philippa.

The conversation between the two women is believed to have involved something along these lines. Joan spoke to Isabella and said, *"Isabella, I believe that it shall be in the best interests of both Hainault and England as well as the French provinces of Aquitaine and Ponthieu for our children to become betrothed to each other. I am suggesting that your son, Edward marries my daughter, and that both of them are betrothed to each other as quickly as we can arrange it!"*

Isabella replied, *"If my son becomes betrothed to your daughter, I shall require a dowry of £28,000 to be paid directly to me and no-one else! So, Joan, what is your answer, shall you and your husband pay me the necessary twenty-eight thousand pounds, or not?"*

Joan replied, *"Isabella, I will strongly put it to William, my husband, that he accepts your proposal to have our children behoved to each other and that he pays you the twenty-eight thousand pounds immediately!"* That was done, and Count William I of Hainault paid the sum of twenty-eight thousand pounds in the form of gold marks to Isabella who was overjoyed by that.

He said, *"There you go, Isabella, here is the agreed dowry for the hand of my daughter Philippa to your son Edward. I know that you badly need money for your planned invasion of England. This dowry should make all of that easier for you! I can supply you with many of the soldiers whom you shall need. I have on hand a spare force of one thousand and five hundred men. Comprising both Germanic and French mercenary soldiers. They are French cavalry and German infantry soldiers Also; I shall be happy to help train your army if you would like that to happen. Other bishops who support the Liberation Army of Isabella are the Bishops of Lincoln and Herford!"*

On the 24th of September 1326, the mercenary army led by Isabella and the 7th Baron of Wigmore Sir Roger Mortimer, landed at Harwick, located on the English coast to the east of Ipswich. Having finally landed upon English soil, Isabella, and Roger Mortimer, pushed on towards Cambridge with their mercenary army, arriving there on the 26th of September 1326.

Isabella and Roger Mortimer were glad that they had the foresight to have messages about the proposed invasion and the crimes of the Edward II and Le Despencer administration spread all over southern England by the three bishops who they had contacted.

The Bishops of Lincoln and Hereford preached to their congregations that Sir Roger Mortimer was aiding Queen Isabella to replace the present administration of King Edward II and le Despenser regime which was bringing ever-more misery to the people of England.

Although the name of Edmund Fitzalan was a new one to English people, they soon learned to fear and to hate him as much as Hugh Le Despencer the Elder and the Younger. All three of them were plundering the treasury of England!

Isabella Makes a Proclamation at Wallingford

Thanks to the sedition of England which had been organised by Isabella and Roger Mortimer with the bishops resulting in many people flocking to the side of Isabella and her little army, her army quickly became both large and efficient. That allowed her to take Cambridge quickly and easily.

Her disgust and hate of both Hugh Le Despencer the Elder and the Younger was driving her relentlessly forward. She resolved to proclaim at Wallingford; *"For those of you who do not know me, I shall introduce myself! I am your Queen Isabella, and I am putting right the past wrongs inflicted upon you by both my husband, King Edward II, and his administration of both Hugh Le Despencer the Elder and his son, Hugh Le Despencer the Younger as well as the latest addition of Edmund Fitzalan who is actively conspiring the rescuing of my husband, King Edward II and the Le Despencers while they are robbing England of her wealth, which they are taking for their own use!*

I know full-well that the combination of my husband and his administration have been robbing the treasury of England in order to enrich themselves, while they keep on raising ever higher taxes to attempt to have some money in the government coffers which they have emptied!

I have been robbed of my own ancestral lands in both France and England by the greedy practices of both Le Despencers who also took away my own children! I hereby denounced both of them as being guilty of High Treason and I hereby make the announcement that they shall be hunted down and brought to justice!"

The Le Despencers, the King & Edmund Fitzalan Flee Towards Wales

As a result of being fore-warned, King Edward II and the two Le Despencers fled west. They had with them a very large sum of money which they had obtained by emptying the treasury.

As they approached Neath, many of the King's soldiers were talking among themselves. Typical of these conversation was that which occurred between private soldiers Edmund Smith and John Cooper. Edmund said, *"John, I shall not ever again serve King Edward II, or his poofter chamberlain called Hugh Le Despencer the younger, or for that matter his father called Hugh Le Despencer the Elder! They, as well as the king have been robbing the English people of their wealth and keeping it for themselves! I am going to join Queen Isabella in the fight against her husband, King Edward II, will you join me in doing so?"* John replied, *"Yes, I will join you and I also hope that many others will also desert the king and that will make the task of deposing her husband easier for Isabella!"* And so, most of the army of King Edward II deserted him and he had to flee!

As Isabella and her small army of 1,500 men were going toward Cambridge, after landing at Harwich, Isabella was pleasantly surprised to see her small army was quickly growing much stronger.

Her husband, King Edward II, had ordered the collection of local levies and he tried to mobilise the country of England in order to stop Isabella and Mortimer, but he failed in doing so! The soldiers he mobilised, immediately changed sides and their number were greatly swelled as victims of the Le Despencer regime and their relatives flocked to the cause of Isabella. That was an illustration of just how well the three Bishops had done their work of preparing the English people for civil war.

As time went on and Isabella's army swept inland to Cambridge. In Cambridge, her army was joined by Thomas, Earl of Norfolk and Henry, Earl of Leicester. He was the brother of the late Thomas, Earl of Lancaster, who had been hanged along with Baron de Clifford by King Edward II. As well, present was Thomas the new Earl of Lancaster who was Isabella's uncle.

He announced, *"I and all of my army, and the family members of my soldiers are today, the 27th of September 1326, moving south to join Queen Isabella's war against the Le Despencer regime! Let no-one doubt the resolve of my soldiers and me! We are resolute and we shall obtain total victory for Isabella to rule England!"*

As usual, the rumour mill was spewing out gossip which included some factual statements, and also much misinformation. Both Mortimer and Isabella encouraged the rumour mill to engage this sort of gossip as it was sure to reach the ears of King Edward II and his regime of the Le Despencers and Edmund

Fitzalan. It should be pointed out that Edmund Fitzallan was entirely innocent of the charges levelled against him by Roger Mortimer. Mortimer had started rumours the Edmund was planning to rescue King Edward II so that Mortimer could obtain his wealth and his lands.

On the 27th of September, a messenger was escorted to King Edward II. Approaching the seated king, the messenger prostrated himself at Edward's feet. Edward raised him up and spoke to him. He said, *"Yes, messenger, what is it?"* The messenger replied, *"Your majesty, England has been invaded by a foreign force with a strength of 1,500 men under the command of your Queen Isabella and Sir Roger Mortimer! They have already taken the coastal areas near Harwich, and they have successfully occupied both Cambridge and Oxford.*

Although they only started with 1,500 men, their army has grown to six times that number by English people who have been victims of the Le Despencers and their families joining Isabella and Sir Roger Mortimer! They are currently marching towards London!"

King Edward II said, *Messenger, you have done well! Now go and refresh before you resume your duties!"* Next, Edward called for his personal guard. Upon the guard commander approaching him, Edward said, *"Sergeant, take a group of ten of your men and go to the local sheriffs, including Richard de Perrers, the High Sheriff of Essex. Instruct him to immediately mobilise armed opposition against Isabella and Sir Roger Mortimer."* Edward's sergeant in command of his personal guard detachment tried to carry-out Edward's orders to him. Here is what happened.

As the Sergeant and his men were being escorted to see High Sherrif Richard de Perrers, the high sheriff was seated at a table eating pork and drinking wine. The soldiers who were escorting Edward's men said, *"Sir, this is a detachment of the King's guard! Their sergeant is in command, and he has asked to have an audience with you sir!"* De Perrers said, *"Very well, let us all hear what it is that the king wants now!"*

The sergeant in command of the King's Guard said, *"Sir, his majesty, King Edward II has commanded that you and the other local sheriffs are to mobilise armed opposition to the advancing armies of Isabella and the traitor called Sir Roger Mortimer!"* The High Sheriff laughed. Then he said, *"Sergeant, I have no quarrel with you or your men. You are free to go as you may like! In fact, I have instructed my kitchen staff to serve you all hot meals before you leave here for return to King Edward II!*

The condition of your release from here is that you take my answer to the orders of King Edward II to him and ensure that he both gets my answer and that he understands it completely! You say that the King has ordered that I and the other sheriffs of Essex and surrounding areas must mobilise everyone for the defence of the King! That shall not happen! Neither myself or my fellow sheriffs shall pay homage to a shirt lifting poofter who is so far up the arseholes of other men that he is useless as a king and soldier! Tell that poor excuse for a man that he is now on his own!"

The sergeant replied, *"Very good sir, I shall do as you have instructed me!"* That was followed by the sergeant and his men having their hot meals and then returning to King Edward II. As the sergeant and his men were being escorted in to see King Edward II, he said, *"Well sergeant, how did it go?"* The sergeant answered, *"Badly your majesty! We delivered your orders to the sheriffs as you ordered, but they all laughed at us! As for the High Sheriff of Essex called Richard de Perrers, he openly told us to go away and that you have no authority. He also said that he is on the side of Queen Isabella and Sir Roger Mortimer!"*

More Soldiers Desert King Edward II

Private soldier Gerard Smith was speaking to his companion. He said, *"Robert, I have been told by many people that we are supporting a king who is about to be well and truly beaten! There is much public anger that the King Edward II and his Le Despencer Administration has been systematically robbing the treasury and given riches and land to the Le Despencer family!*

Also, the people are doing without and there is a general uprising occurring! That is being helped by the invasion of England by Queen Isabella and her army! I do not know about you, but I for one, am deserting the King and his poofter lover! He and his poofter lover can deal with the situation entirely on their own!"

Due to the attitudes of his own soldiers being like that, most of the armed force of King Edward II and the two Le Despencer men, deserted their posts. London was quickly becoming unsafe for many people due to the unrest and what was a prelude to civil war. Edward was alarmed that the degree of unrest was such that no-one could guarantee his safety. Isabella and her rapidly growing army moved to the west again and finally reached Oxford on the 2nd of October 1326. Soon after she had taken the city, she called a meeting of the city's aldermen and addressed them.

She said, *"My people of Oxford, you are suffering from the administration of Hugh Le Despencer the Elder and his son called Hugh Le Despencer the Younger have been brought to my attention! I have issued warrants for the arrest and bringing to trial for crimes of High Treason against both men and their current favourite and partner in crime called Edmund Fitzalan! I urge all of you to inform my soldiers of the where-abouts of these men!"*

Shortly after she had made the speech, a man was escorted into her presence. He had been very insistent that he be given an audience with the queen. As the man approached her in the company of ten of her soldiers, Isabella recognised the man.

It was Bishop Adam Orleton, who had been the Bishop of Westminster. With him was the Bishop of Hereford. Realising that this was a golden opportunity for her to get even more people to join her side of the war between her forces and those of the Edward and Le Despencer forces, Isabella loudly spoke while she was within the city market areas, where many people heard her speak. She said, *"Bishop Adam Orleton, the Bishop of Westminster, how lovely to see you again! How are you?"*

Adam Orleton replied, *"My lady, I am well, but very tired and hungry as one becomes when one is hunted by the poofter King of England who commits sodomy with the even more evil two Le Despencer men! I and the bishop of Hereford here, have been in hiding from the Le Despencers ever since you wrote to me to begin preaching against the King and his sodomy loving male friends, Hugh Le Despencer the younger and his queer friend called Edmund Fitzalan! I have been successful in preaching against the king and his supporters such that you shall very soon have an even bigger army than you currently have! That is why I am being hunted by the evil Le Despencers!"*

Isabella was overjoyed by that. She said, *"Your Grace, Adam Orleton, Bishop of Westminster, I truly thank you for your great support of my movement to free England of the Edward and Le Despencer administration! In order for the population to even more be on our side; I want you to go to the university here in Oxford and give a public lecture about the evils of the Le Despencers! Please do so immediately!"*

That was done, and it resulted in even more people flocking to join the fight against the Edward-Le Despencer administration. Isabella now asked Bishop Adam Orleton, *"Adam, I have been chasing the Le Despencer men and Edmund Fitzallan for a long time, but they always seem to be ahead of me somehow! Do you know where they may be?* He replied, *"Isabella, it has come to my attention that King Edward II and Hugh Le Despencer the Younger have fled to the west, and it appears that they may be going towards Wales!*

Also, I have reports that stating that Hugh Le Despencer the Elder is in Bristol where he hopes to be able to stop you and your consort of Sir Roger Mortimer from advancing any further! Also, I have it on excellent authority that you now have the support and backing of all surviving family members of Lancaster family of Earls! That simply means that you have an effective alliance with the Lancasters to oppose Edward and the Le Despencers!"

Isabella and her army pushed southwards towards London. While so doing, they paused at Dunstable on the 7th of October. Civil disorder was rife, and London was in the hands of mobs who hunted down anyone they thought was a royalist and therefore, on the sides of Edward II and the le Despencers.

Bishop Walter de Stapleton did not realise the extent to which royal power had collapsed in London. When he saw that rioters were threatening his property in London, He issued orders to his private army members to protect his property and interfere against the supporters of Isabella with military action.

He yelled out to his commander of soldiers, *"Using crossbows and long bows, kill all rioters that try to come onto my property!"* Sir Blaxland was in command of his private army, and he answered, *"Sir, the men and I can attempt to hold back the mob while you escape, however the mob outside of these walls is* large and getting both larger and more violent all of the time! Please allow me to suggest that you get out of here now while you still can!"

However, Bishop Walter de Stapleton misjudged just how hated he was and that resulted in his downfall! He was attacked and killed. His head was sent to Isabella as a gift from her supporters! Meanwhile, Edward was still fleeing towards the west. He finally reached Gloucester on the 9th of October. Isabella was informed of that, and she spoke to Roger Mortimer.

She said, *"Roger, I know that Edward reached Gloucester on the 9th of October! You and the army are to respond by quickly marching west towards Gloucester in an attempt to cut him off!"* Roger and the army did so and reached Gloucester a week later. Meanwhile, Edward managed to slip across the border into Wales on the same day. The army of Isabella grew considerably because it was joined by the northern barons led by Thomas Wake, Henry de Beaumont, and Henry Percy. That now gave Isabella the numerical advantage!

Isabella and Her Army Besiege Bristol

Hugh Le Despencer the Elder continued to hold out in Bristol against the forces of Isabella and Sir Roger Mortimer. A knight who had been leading his platoon sized force of men against the walls of Bristol, was in a hurry to confer with Queen Isabella about the attack on the city. He attempted to gain an audience with her, but he was repeatedly refused that. Finally acting upon his own sense of desperation, he shouted at the members of the Queen's Guard. He shouted, *"Oh you fucking fools! You are withholding me from doing my duty of informing the Queen that there is a simple solution to her taking of Bristol! When she is told that you fucking halfwits refused to let me see her on urgent business regarding her attack upon Bristol, you will lose your ugly heads! I strongly suggest that you let me see her immediately!"*

A sergeant of the Queen's Guard stepped forward and spoked to the knight! He said, *"Sir, I am Sergeant Brad Morris of Queen Isabella's Guard. I understand that you are having some trouble with my sub-ordinates, who appear to be giving you some grief sir! In order to rectify the situation, how can I and my men be of service to you, sir?"*

Sir Antony de Silver said, *"Thank you sergeant, it is pleasant to see that at least you have some common sense around here! It appears to me that your soldiers have none of it at all! Please immediately escort me to see Queen Isabella on a matter of grave importance!"*

Sergeant Brad Morris said, *"Worry not sir, I shall personally escort you in to see her along with two of my best men!"* That was quickly arranged, and the meeting between Sir Antony de Silver and Queen Isabella quickly took place.

Isabella was sitting upon a throne when Sir Antony de Silver was escorted into her presence. She looked closely at him and decided that she liked what she saw. Sir Antony prostrated himself at Isabella's feet and she raised him up. She said, *"I understand that you wish to speak to me sir knight on matters of grave importance to me. So, sir knight, please introduce yourself to me and then tell me what it is that you consider to be so important!"*

Sir Antony de Silver replied, *"Your majesty, I am Sir Antony de Silver. During attacks or forays into and around Bristol on your behalf, I have noticed that the city only has limited supplies of water! I feel that you should exploit that and put into place a siege of Bristol from the 18th of October for as long as it takes for the defenders to give up the fight due to a lack of fresh water!*

Also, your majesty, I have actually been in contact with the man whom you are seeking in Bristol, Hugh Le Despencer the Elder! He told me to point out to you that he is holding both of your daughters, Eleanor of Woodstock, and Joan of the Tower! I know that if you put into place the siege of Bristol immediately, you will very quickly have the ultimate victory and Hugh Le Despencer the Elder will become your prisoner! You shall be able to have the victory and the hated Le Despencer the Elder held as a prisoner without getting a great number of casualties among your own soldiers! So please, your majesty, order the immediate encirclement and siege of Bristol now!"

The siege of Bristol was put into place with the result that the city fell on the 26th of October. Hugh Le Despencer the Elder was quickly found and made a prisoner. Meanwhile, Edward and his favourite, Hugh Le Despencer the Younger, tried to sail to Lundy, which is a small island just off the coast near Devon. Instead of easily getting away they had to turn back towards the areas they had left in Wales, due to rough weather.

Isabella Orders Henry of Lancaster to Arrest Her Husband

Now that she had Bristol secured and Hugh Le Despencer the Elder in custody awaiting trial, Isabella sent for Henry of Lancaster to come to her while she was in Hereford. Hereford being a border town close to Wales. After two days, Henry of Lancaster was escorted into the presence of Queen Isabella.

As Henry was escorted into her presence, and he prostrated himself before her. She said, *"Arise Henry of Lancaster, my friend, we have much to discuss!"* Henry arose and Isabella said, *"Henry, I have a special mission for you! I need you to locate and arrest my husband, who is currently King Edward II! He will not be so for much longer, because as soon as I arrive in London, I shall convene Parliament and Edward shall be stripped of his commission to rule as king in favour of his son and mine who is also called Edward!*

My son is currently aged thirteen years and so, I shall rule as his regent until he is old enough to rule in his own right! You are not to harm my husband and you shall give him the respect normally given to a king! I want you to let my husband have freedom of movement within Kenilworth Castle, which you own!

I also want you to allow him to leave the castle grounds for up to two days once every third month under escort. His escort must see to it that he cannot ever organise armed resistance to the rule of his son, who shall become known as King Edward III! So, Henry, my friend, are you clear on what you must do?"

Henry the Earl of Lancaster said, "Yes, your majesty! Have no fear! I shall track down your husband and take him to my Kenilworth Castle where he shall stay unless he is on one of his allowed visits out of the castle! Your majesty, it is now the 30th of October, and it could be some weeks before I and my forces can locate and arrest your husband. I shall start my forces looking for him in the south of Wales! I have heard that he could be somewhere to the west of Llantrisant, so my men shall begin their search for him in that area!"

King Edward II continued to elude Isabella and her men until he and Hugh Le Despencer the Younger were seen going into a large stone cottage near Llantrisant on the 16th of November by a private soldier in the army of the Earl of Lancaster.

Private Peter Woods approached his immediate superior, Sergeant Moore and spoke to him. He said, *"Sergeant, I have seen two men whom I believe are the fugitives we are seeking, namely the poofter king Edward and his bum chum called Hugh Le Despencer the Younger! I saw the two of them go into a large stone cottage near Llantrisant!"* Sergeant Moore reacted by saying, *"Very good Private Woods! Our commander shall be well pleased by this!"*

The sergeant went to his commander and told him what Private woods had seen and where. The commander reacted by going directly to the commander of the Lancaster cavalry force and told him. That resulted in a squadron of cavalry riding toward the stone cottage. As the squadron got closer to the cottage, Sir Andrew de Halla commanding the squadron called a halt to its progress. He ordered, *"Dismount gentlemen, we shall cover the remaining distance on foot! That way we will not give away the fact that we are coming to the king and his poofter lover!"* So, they all dismounted, and two men were left with the horses while the remainder of the squadron walked silently towards the stone cottage which was visible just on the horizon.

As the group of men got closer to the cottage, Andrew de Halla quietly ordered, *"Men, you are to completely surround the cottage! We must make sure that the men inside it cannot escape! You are all to make sure that the King comes to no harm! On the other hand, you can be as rough and cruel as you like to the King's favourite poofter! I do not care how much you make him suffer. The king is not to be molested by order of Queen Isabella! Do you all understand your orders?"* That was followed by the men saying, *"Yes sir!"*

With the cottage now surrounded, Andrew de Halla ordered, *"Men, we are going to firstly try to move into the cottage without making any noise which will give away our intent to the King! So, quietly, open the door for us and move into the cottage!"* That was quickly and quietly done. As the armed soldiers were moving into the cottage, they could all see King Edward was having anal sex with Hugh Le Despencer the Younger. Despite his disgust at what he was seeing Sir Andrew de Halla loudly yelled, *"Your majesty, King Edward II and Hugh Le Despencer the Younger, you* are both under arrest upon the orders of Queen Isabella acting upon the behalf of the people of England!"

King Edward II immediately accepted his fate and surrendered, while Hugh Le Despencer the Younger tried to put up a fight. That delighted the armed soldiers who were arresting both men. As a result Hugh was badly injured from being knocked about by the soldiers who were taking a great delight in assaulting someone whom they considered to be a *"Shirt lifting poofter!"*

As the soldiers took great delight in being rude and assaulting Hugh Le Despencer the Younger, their commanding sergeant Ralf Becket calmed the situation by commanding his men. He said, *"That is quite enough of your disgusting behaviour towards a prisoner! You are calling him a shirt lifting poofter and maybe he is that! However, you are members of the Queens Guard of Queen Isabella and as such, you are responsible for the safety of that man until such time as he has been tied and found guilty of crimes.*

Until that happens, he must be presumed to be innocent of all charges against him! All of you shall cease to assault him and from now on, you shall all protect the man, no matter if you like that or not. For that is the English way and it is expected you shall comply!"

That having been said, the sergeant spoke to Hugh Le Despenser the Younger. He said, *"Hugh Le Despencer the Younger, in the name of her majesty Queen Isabella of England, I am charging you with the crimes of high treason and sodomy! You have the right to remain silent, and you do not have to say anything, but everything that you do say, shall be written down and later used against you in a court of English law! So, Hugh Le Despencer the Younger, do you understand your rights?"*

Hugh Le Despencer the Younger remained silent. The sergeant said to his men, *"Corporal Smith, you and private Jenkins shall ride to Queen Isabella and then you shall inform her that we have the fugitive Hugh Le Despencer the Younger in our custody and that we await her orders!"*

When the news of the arrest of Hugh Le Despencer the Younger was received by Isabella she was overjoyed! She said, *"And so, finally, we have the monster who corrupted the morals and the mind of my darling Edward and who kidnapped my children and kept them away from me by letting his father Hugh Le Despencer the Elder keep my son and my daughters in captivity at his foul residence in Bristol!*

Hugh Le Despencer the Elder was tried for his crimes and found guilty of treason very soon after Bristol fell to my army! He has since been taken to Tyburn and hanged in public. His death was not an easy one! When he was hanged, the executioner simply pulled on the rope around his neck and then left Hugh hanging and slowly chocking to death! That gave the onlookers something to be entertained by! The sight of Hugh Le Despencer hanging by his neck kicking and twitching until death claimed him and his body was finally still at the end of the rope around his neck!

I have much more severe plan for Hugh Le Despencer the Younger! When he is found to be guilty, he shall firstly be hanged, but he will be brought down from the gallows before he is dead so that he can be tortured to death! He shall be placed upon a ladder against a wall, and he shall be at a height of fourteen feet above ground level.

There shall be two small fires burning near the foot of the ladder. A torturer shall firstly cut of his testes and throw them upon the fires. That shall be followed by the torturer cutting off his penis and throwing that upon the fire. Then, his fingers and toes shall be cut off! Next Hugh Le Despencer the Younger shall be disembowelled and his guts thrown upon the fires. Next, what is left of his body shall be cut into quarters and they shall be taken to distant parts of England, and Wales in four separate locations and buried there. No-one shall ever know where his body parts are buried! It is necessary to do that in order to prevent the followers of both Le Despencers making martyrs of them and then becoming a problem later on!"

Parliament of the 7th of January 1327

With Edward II and Hugh Le Despencer, the Younger fleeing into Wales, Isabella opened Parliament on the 7th of January 1327. During the opening of the Parliament, she said, *"As many of you already know, I have returned to England in order to ensure that the country is reconstructed from the ground to the top and that justice shall prevail.*

I hereby call upon this parliament to end the commission of my husband, King Edward II as King! I also want you to then appoint his son and my son, Prince Edward, as King Edward III! At the age of thirteen years, he is far too young to rule England as king, therefore, I shall rule as his regent! My consort, Sir Roger Mortimer shall stay in the background, and he will not have any royal power.

Once my husband, King Edward II has been located and arrested, he shall reside at Kenilworth Castle where he shall have relative freedom. He shall not ever rule again. That is now being done by me in so much as I am ruling as the regent for King Edward III until he is old enough to rule in his own right! I have decreed that my husband, Edward shall be allowed out of the castle for up to two days before he must return and report to his administrator, the keeper of the castle, Henry the Earl of Lancaster who shall act as he sees fit on my behalf!"

So it was that the Parliament debated the issue and resolved the Edward II was not fit to rule England. The Parliament also endorsed the son of Edward and Isabella to be the King and that he would become known as King Edward III! So it was that Edward III was crowned in January of 1327. (he ruled for the next fifty years).

However, that did not entirely suit Isabella or her lover Sir Roger Mortimer who now plotted to keep the thirteen-year-old King Edward a prisoner within his own castle and palace! Both Isabella and Roger Mortimer saw to it that King Edward III could not rule, and they illegally ruled in his stead as regents while keeping him as a prisoner. Something that both Isabella and Sir Roger Mortimer forgot about was that King Edward II was in fact a loving father who had the love and respect of his children. That was something which would aid King Edward III later on.

The Teenage King Thinks that he Saw Something

A few days later, Isabella and her son, Edward were riding together near Kenilworth Castle when the young Edward III suddenly said, *"Mother, look over there, is that my father?"* Isabella looked in the direction pointed out by her son, and she saw nothing. Accordingly, she said, *"My son, I have no idea what you think you just saw, but there is nothing there now. Anyway, it could not be your father, because he is confined to Kenilworth Castle for the foreseeable future!"*

And so, the two people rode on. Then, just after Isabella had stopped the riding of herself and her son in order to refresh themselves, her son, Edward III was walking towards a large oak tree when he saw and was spoken to by his father, the ex-king Edward II.

The ex-king said, *"My son, do not be alarmed! For I shall always be on your side! You are now the king, and I shall aid you to become the king that you can and should be. The lover of your mother, called Sir Roger Mortimer is exploiting the situation brought about by my fall from grace. Every so often, I get to leave Kenilworth Castle and it is on those occasions* that I can offer you my counsel in matters of government if you are interested.

You are going to have many problems brought about by the ambitions of Isabella and Sir Roger Mortimer who are presently messing about in Scotland, yet another country where they have no business to be! Mark my words, my son, that soon, England shall face renewed war with the Scots under the leadership of their new king called Robert de Bruce! I am going back to Kenilworth Castle now, and I shall again seek you to have a tactical discussion with you in three months at the most from now! So my son, keep this meeting between us entirely to yourself! For if others find out about it, you can bet that Sir Roger Mortimer shall kill you!"

The young King Edward III said, *"Thank you, my father! For a long time now, I have been feeling as if I am a prisoner within my own palace. That fits in exactly with what you have told me! So, I look forward to our next meeting, which I shall make easier for you by visiting you at Kenilworth Castle in my own right! I can arrange visit for me to see you at Kenilworth because I am on friendly terms with the owner of the castle, the Earl of Lancaster!*

I am completely fed up with the activity of both my mother and Sir Roger Mortimer who are in my view embarking upon the bankrupting of England due to the extravagances of them both! Take care and travel safely my father! I shall call upon you at Kenilworth Castle by the middle of the next three months in order to confer with you about the developing situation regarding the adventures of my mother and Sir Roger Mortimer in Scotland!" With those words spoken, both men resumed their journeys towards their homes.

Edward III Overhears Plotting by his Mother and Mortimer

Edward was kept away from all power, and he was only allowed to accompany Roger Mortimer while Mortimer was fighting the Scots so that Mortimer could keep an eye upon what the teenage king was doing. During one night, the teenage king could not sleep, and he began to wander about Windsor Castle where he, his mother and Mortimer were living.

As he was walking toward an annex located on the west wing of the castle, he could clearly hear Isabella and Roger Mortimer speaking. He hear Isabella saying, *"Roger, we must completely reign in all spending! There is only £46 left in the treasury! Your insatiable desires for riches are getting to the point where England shall soon be bankrupt and then, total anarchy shall be the final result! Much of this has been forced upon us by your failed adventures in Scotland, where you failed in your objective of bringing the Scots to heel! Instead, it is you who has been beaten and now England must pay!"*

The teenage king did not like what he had heard, and he resolved to discuss the situation with his father, Edward II at Kenilworth Castle. He therefore sneaked out of Windsor and rode his horse to Kenilworth castle where he had an audience with the Earl of Lancaster.

Lancaster said, *"What is it that I can do for you your majesty?"* Edward replied, *"It is necessary for me to confer with my father, the former King Edward II! There are many problems facing England and I must get my father's advice on how best to handle the situation. I also would very much like you to be present during our discussions Earl Lancaster!*

So with Earl Lancaster leading the way, the teenage King Edward III was taken to his father, who immediately embraced him. Edward the son, spoke to his father and Earl Lancaster. He said, *"Gentlemen, I have overheard discussions between my mother and Roger Mortimer! Things are grim and the royal treasury only has £46 left in it! Apparently, those who are governing this country in my name have no idea of financial matters! They have jointly completed what was started by the Le Despencers when they just took money and lands for themselves without any thought as to how things would be paid for!*

As a result, my mother is expecting my sister called Joan of the Tower (because she was born in the Tower of London) to become the wife of the Scottish King! My father and Earl Lancaster, please help me to come up with ideas as to how to stop these awful events from happening!"

The former King Edward II had by now joined his son and Lancaster. The ex-king Edward II said, *"Son, please be patient and work towards becoming the actual king by arresting Sir Roger Mortimer when the time for that is right! Be aware that your mother is ever-watchful, and you can expect a lot of trouble from* her if she suspects that you are somehow going to take away the power that she and Roger Mortimer are exercising over you! I see that you already have Lancaster here on your side! I think that you need to build upon that!

You need more alliances with the English nobility to support you! I would like to see you use the support of Earl Lancaster to expand your influence. After that has grown to a point where you feel that you have the advantage and that you are holding necessary power, go to the bed-chamber of Isabella and Roger Mortimer and arrest both of them!"

Isabella and Mortimer in Scotland

A Scottish war of Independence took place involving England and Scotland beginning in March 1296 when Edward I (Longshanks) invaded Scotland, resulting in the sacking, and burning Berwick as part of his invasion of Scotland. By 1323, England was ruled by King Edward II. The English forces were completely expelled from Scotland and the Scots were then ruled by Robert de Bruce. He carried out several raids into England, while English pirates were devastating Scottish shipping.

The very young King Edward III was silently walking about Windsor Palace at night when he overheard Sir Roger Mortimer and his mother, Isabella conferring. Isabella said, *"Roger, we must do something about the Scots under the command of Robert de Bruce causing chaos and raiding deep into our country of England! I need you to attack the Scots, using my large army and you must bring those barbarians to heel!*

Be sure to rid my England of all of those vile invaders and barbaric people who would harm our country! I have heard that the leader of the Scots called Robert de Bruce, has led a force of Scots invading England! Apparently, there is a large Scottish force of ten thousand men being led by Donald, the Earl of Mar, Thomas the Earl of Moray, and James the lord of Douglas!

I have been told that the Scots have very little in the way of supply trains and that they disperse over large sections of countryside in order to forage and that is how they feed themselves while in the field! That practice of being able to 'Live off the Land with the assistance of the People' gives the Scots a high degree of mobility and operational effectiveness! The effectiveness of the Scots is such that they have plundered and burned their way south and they are near Appleby now! I find that to be a most unsuitable situation for England!

I command you to take my army stationed at York and you are to move against the Scots by the 1st of July 1327! You must see to it that the Scots are taught not to invade England again!"

Roger Mortimer replied, *"Isabella, my love, by my moving out against the Scots on the 1st of July, it should give England the advantage because the equipment of our armies is much better than that of the Scots!*

Also, there is the current and continuing problem of how to ensure that your son by your husband of King Edward II learns his place and never tries to interfere with our government of England! In order to make sure that he shall be compliant for the rest of his life, I wish to take him along on the campaign against the Scots! That way, he shall at least see some of the things that happen in war!" Isabella replied, *"Very well, then Roger, you have my approval to take my son with you when you move against the Scots!"*

What Isabella did not know was that Roger Mortimer had organised a meeting with a section of English infantry (men at arms). Corporal Robert Smythe went to the tent of Mortimer while he was with the English army at York. After being escorted in to see Mortimer, Robert Smythe spoke. He said, *"I understand that you wish to see me, my lord!"*

Sir Roger Mortimer replied, *"We are moving out to engage the Scots in battle! By the 3rd of August, I am confident that the English army shall penetrate as far as the south bank of the River Wear! When we arrive there, we shall not engage the Scots in battle, we shall simply watch them and wait for them to try a move against our superior and better equipped forces!*

So, assuming that all goes to plan, and this army takes possession of the south bank of the River Wear by the 3rd of August, I have a special operation for you and your ten men! You and your section are to wait within the English Camp until the middle of the night. I have organised with the Scots that they shall attack the English camp then! They are sending some small units to disrupt our English camp!

As soon as you hear the activity caused by the Scottish raiders, you and your section are to go to the middle of our camp and locate the tent of King Edward III who is aged between fourteen and fifteen years! You and your men must locate the guy lines holding up the tent of the king. You must then cause the entire tent to fall upon the young king! Make sure that you also loudly yell in Scottish accents that you are going to kill the Sassenach King, but do not hurt him, just scare the living daylights out of him! That way he should become more manageable by me!"

So Robert Smythe and his section did as they had been ordered by Sir Roger Mortimer. They waited until they could hear the Scots rampaging through the English camp. With Corporal Smythe leading, they located and cut the guy lines holding up the tent of the king, which now collapsed over him.

Things did not go completely to the wishes of Roger Mortimer. King Edward III, although he was now only in his fifteenth year, was unafraid and he quickly recovered his composure. Having done so, he immediately began to issue orders for the defence of the English camp and the Scottish raiders were driven off, and they returned to their own camp!

Edward and his platoon sized unit were patrolling near the south bank of the River Wear when the English forward scout noticed that a man who was armed, and alone was making his way to the north. He silently raised his right hand in a signal to stop.

The column stopped and he then touched the top of his head and followed that with patting his left shoulder. That was the silent signal saying, *'Send the commander to me!"* King Edward III rode to the forward scout and said, *"Scout, you have summoned me, what is it that is so important?"* The scout replied, *"Your majesty, there toward the north, is a man who is bound to have important information about the Scots!"* Edward said, *"Thank you scout, we shall take him prisoner and then we shall find out what is going on!"*

The man was apprehended and interrogated. The interrogation revealed that the Scots were going to move their entire army that night. Edward took the intelligence to the de-facto ruler of England, Sir Roger Mortimer. When Edward told Mortimer of the Scottish plans.

Mortimer said, *"Well, Edward, I did not consider you to have enough balls to do what you have done on this campaign! In the light of your information, it appears that the Scots are out of food and that they shall try to take the food held by our English army! I have therefore ordered that many bonfires be lighted all over the English position! I want the Scots to attack us! If they do so, they shall die!"*

The reality of the situation was that the Scots were indeed out of food. Far from being leadless or disorganised, they picked their way through a swamp which the English considered to be impassable. After having silently navigated their way through the swamp, the Scots continued their journey to the north, even though they were laden with plunder taken from the English!

When they heard about it, the opinion of the English people about the entire Scottish campaign was, *"It is to the great shame and dishonour and to the scorn of all of England that we, the English people consider the regents called Isabella and Sir Roger Mortimer to be totally incompetent and never to be trusted! Due to the insatiable greed of Isabela and Mortimer, England shall soon be bankrupt! There is only forty-seven pounds left in the treasury! The administration of Isabella and Roger Mortimer is much worse than the previous administration of King Edward II and the Le Despencers!"*

The Aftermath

I often wonder about those who wish to use mercenary forces and yet, never consider that the mercenaries must not only be paid, but that they must be paid on time! As well, because the north of England had been systematically looted, extensive tax concessions had to be granted. These things combined and with an annual income of seventy thousand pounds (£70,000) being dropped to thirty thousand pounds (£30,000) the treasury found itself in great difficulty.

The mercenaries hired by Isabella and Sir Roger Mortimer submitted a bill for forty-one thousand pounds (£41,000) which was more than the entire income for the year because of the tax concessions. It is well known that wars cost money, even if the country having the war does not use mercenary soldiers. Things were now so bad for English forces that they were not able to go out of their base at Alnwick. In 1328, the English lacked the money to be able to raise soldiers to oppose the Scots. This caused Isabella and Sir Roger Mortimer to negotiate.

The Treaty of Edinburgh – Northampton

Peace talks were regularly held between 1321 and 1324. They resulted in little to no progress being made. Before he was deposed as king, Edward II allowed English privateers to attack Flemish and Scottish ships trading between the two countries. He however, claimed that he did not allow pirates to operate out of England, which is one of the things that Hugh Le Despencer the Younger was tried and executed for.

An example of the privateers (English Government backed and tolerated pirates operating against known enemies of England) was the privateers seizing the Flemish ship *Pelarym* which was considered to be worth £2,000 and murdering all Scots on board it! Frustrated at the English actions, Robert de Bruce demanded justice, but to no avail! He therefore invaded Ireland and renewed the Auld alliance with France, which was concluded in on the 26th of April 1326 and called the Treaty of Corbel which was signed and sealed in Corbel, France.

Isabella and Sir Roger Mortimer were during this time quickly proving themselves to be no better at administration then King Edward II had been! In fact, they were proving that they were so much worse than the administration headed by Edward II! Due to their quests of not only helping themselves to the vast estates and riches of both of the Le Despencers, but they also both overspent money without a thought of how to replace it!

The negotiations of the Treaty of Edinburgh – Northampton were carried out by Isabella and Roger Mortimer, who said that they were governing England on behalf of the underage King Edward III, of England. On the 1st of March 1328, at a Parliament was held at York, King Edward III issued letters which set the agreement.

Terms of the Treaty

In the treaty, Isabella and Roger Mortimer agreed to renounce all sovereignty over Scotland. Joan, the six-year-old sister of Edward III, was promised in marriage to the son of the Scottish King Robert de Bruce. His name was David, and he was four years old at the time of the betrothal. The Scots agreed to pay England £20,000. It was paid, and immediately squandered by Isabella and Mortimer. It was also agreed that if the marriage should fail, that Scotland would pay another £100,000 to England.

Although King Edward III, agreed to return the *Stone of Destiney* to Scotland, it was not done until 668 years later. It was returned to Scotland, arriving at Edinburgh Castle on the 30th of November 1996. With it came the agreement that it would be transported to England for use in the coronations of subsequent monarchs. The first of these shall be the coronation of King Charles III. (2023).

King Edward III Gathers Strength

Remembering what he had been told by his father in the presence of Earl Lancaster, the young King Edward quickly built up his support among the English nobility. He strongly resented being regaled to a role where he had no power, and was kept in seclusion, becoming little more than a prisoner of his mother and her lover, Sir Roger Mortimer and he resolved that soon after his sixteenth birthday, to rectify the situation.

Edward III was thinking, *"Very well, Sir Roger Mortimer, you have wormed your way into my mother's heart, and now, here you are, keeping my people enslaved while you have the unmitigated hide to take what does not belong to you and you are enriching yourself at the expense of the common people and the nobility of England!"*

Edward continued thinking, *"Bloody Mortimer, I do not know how you are doing it, but you have been able to get my mother act against my father, Edward II! The fact that Parliament stripped my father of the right to rule England and passed it on to me means that I am the rightful king even though I am presently aged fourteen years! What I know is that I love my father and I shall be there for him, just as he has always been there for me!*

You and my mother have misgoverned the Scots to the point where Robert de Bruce is now their king and a capable military commander, unlike bloody Roger Mortimer!" Having had those thoughts, the teenage king who was being held prisoner began to brood over what he should do about the situation and how to do it.

As a result of those deliberations, he resolved to (1) See his father and confer with him as how best to proceed with getting his kingdom of England out of the clutches of Isabela and Sir John Mortimer. (2) make contact with as many other nobles in England as possible and obtain their allegiance. (3) Personally see these nobles and explain the situation of England now being almost bankrupt due to unrestricted spending by his mother and Mortimer!

Suspecting that Isabella and Mortimer would shift his father to a different location, the young teenage in-name-only king sought out some of the staff who were looking after the horses for Isabella and Roger Mortimer. He approached a stable-hand called John Jenkins. He said, *"John Jenkins, I have an important and lucrative job for you to fulfill! If you serve me well, you shall be richly rewarded!"*

John Jenkins answered, *"Thank you, sir, for giving me this opportunity to better myself! What is it that you want me to do?"* Young Edward replied, *"I know that my mother and Roger Mortimer are seeing to it that I am a virtual prisoner within my own palace and within my own camp if I were to ride in support of them! I must have the counsel, of my father so that I can be clear on what it is that I must do in rule to stop their misgoverning of my country!*

I have been told that England is heading towards becoming bankrupt and that can only be due to the way that my mother and Sir Roger Mortimer are plundering the estates of the Le Despencers and all of their followers. There is the added problem of too many exemptions from tax resulting in too little tax money being collected! As well, people are not being compensated for what was done to them by the Le Despencer and Edmund Fitzalan administrations of my father. So, John Jenkins, are you willing to serve me, the rightful king of England?"

John Jenkins replied, *"I shall support you in your endeavours to regain your crown and authority my king! If you wish to ride to Kenilworth Castle to see your father, why not do so in about one hour from now when it is dark? If you were to ride that mare and I rode the gelding next to her, you would be able to discuss things with your father tonight. Now is the ideal time to do this sort of thing because both your mother and Sir Roger Mortimer are in Nottingham attending Parliamentary function. We can see your father and be back here before anyone at all misses us! After we have spoken to your father, it shall be high time for you to personally see other nobles and to obtain their support, sir!"*

The Captive Edward III Sees His Father

Arriving at Kenilworth Castle, the young Edward III, sought out the Earl of Lancaster who owned it. Finally locating him, Edward said, *"Henry, I have the urgent need to speak to my father who is being held here in Kenilworth Castle in 'Protective Custody'."*

Henry the Earl of Lancaster said, *"Very well, Edward, I shall take you to him!"* Two guards wearing the coat of arms of the house of Lancaster appeared, and Edward was escorted into the presence of his father, who was waiting for him in his bedroom on the upper floor of the accommodation part of the castle. As his son was being escorted toward him, Edward II called out, *"Nice to see you again, my son, although I am well treated and allowed to leave the castle here once every two months to three months, I hate this confinement, which is necessary for my own safety! What can I do for you?"*

His son, Edward III said, *"Father, I have been getting some disturbing reports about my mother and Sir Roger Mortimer plotting to move you from here to Berkely Castle, where it has been said, that either Roger Mortimer shall try to kill you or else some of his puppets and allies will do that for him!"*

That prompted his father, the former King Edward II to say, *"My son, remember how I told you a long time ago, that you may have to seize the moment by acting against Isabella and Roger Mortimer while they are at a function? Well son, you have told me that your mother and Roger Mortimer are presently at Nottingham attending a function there because they have to be attending the Parliament. It appears to me that if you were to go to the rooms that have been assigned to them and arrest both of them, you could then seize the power of King that is rightfully yours!*

So, my son, I urge you to consider that instead of riding back to where you have just come from, that you go to where Isabella and Roger Mortimer are and arrest the both of them! I realise that you have no wish to arrest your own mother, but that is something you shall have to do if you want to rule as king! Also, once you have arrested both of them, I suggest that you make your mother the dowager queen and confine her to the grounds of her castle."

Unbeknown to the Former King Edward II, his enemy of Roger Mortimer was actively organising the permanent removal of King Edward II. Roger spoke to his lover, Isabella. He said, *"Isabella, I have organised for a small group of volunteers to go to Kenilworth Castle and return with you husband! I am having him taken to more secure grounds before he and Lancaster can get organised! Once he is imprisoned at Berkley Castle, he shall be much easier to control!"*

Isabella responded by saying, *"What is it about the word "No" that you do not understand Roger? You shall never harm him, for he remains my 'Dear Heart'! If he is hurt in any way, you shall have to reckon with my fury! Do you understand me?"* Sir Roger Mortimer was seething in anger at what Isabella had told him, but he said nothing.

Nothing is so complete a disaster as a jealous person who so despises others that he will stop at nothing in order to bring the person he hates down! That is how Mortimer felt about the former King Edward II! Partly due to the love that Isabella was openly expressing for Edward and also because he wanted Edward completely out of the way, Sir Roger Mortimer called for his team of henchmen and cut-throats.

When Simon Weatherston reported to Roger Mortimer, he said, *"Simond, I have a problem called Ex-king Edward II! Soon he shall be imprisoned at*

Berkley Castle! As soon as you can after he arrives at Berley, you and your men must kill him! He is far too great an embarrassment for us to allow him to live!"

Simond called upon his gang of cut-throats, and they all travelled to Berkley Castle. Upon arrival there, Simond Weatherstone spoke to the owner of the castle. He said, *"Sir, I am Simond Weatherston, and these men are my helpers! We are here upon direct orders from Sir Roger Mortimer! He had ordered the immediate killing of the ex-king Edward II. We are to do the job and then we must return to London with the head of Edward II!"* They were told to proceed, and they killed Edward II and cut off his head for later presentation to Sir Roger Mortimer!

Having done so, they put the head into a saddlebag and returned to London. Upon seeing Roger Mortimer again, Simond Weatherstone presented him with the saddlebag containing the head. Simond said, *"There you are, Sir Roger Mortimer, in the saddlebag is the head of the ex-king Edward II!"*

Unbeknown to them, they had been observed by Isabella who now knew that her husband whom she still loved, had been killed by Sir Roger Mortimer and his gang of cut-throats! She was shaken by that, and she silently resolved, *"Roger, you were told on numerous occasions, to never hurt my "Dear Heart"! However, I have overheard you plotting to kill him! Very well then, if murder is what you want, then you shall have it! I am sick and tired of men and their attitudes by which they consider things to be right for them and to hell with all others! You shall rue the day when you ordered the killing of my Dear Heart!"*

Edward III Arrests his Tormentors!

Isabella opened and presided over a Parliament held in Nottingham during October of 1330. Up until then, the young King Edward III was closely guarded and watched. More and more, he yearned to rule in his own right, so he began to contemplate what he had been told by his father, Edward II, while he was in Kenilworth Castle.

His mother, Isabella spoke to him. She said, *"My good son, It shall soon be time for us to travel to Nottingham where I shall be opening Parliament there and presiding over the proceedings!"* That information excited the young, but disempowered King Edward III.

He began thinking of how to obtain power when he decided, *"It is high time for me to take over governing England in my own right! Neither my mother nor her lover called Sir Roger Mortimer have been officially installed as regents who can rule on my behalf! Therefore, what they are both doing by keeping me back from governing England, as is my due. That can only be seen as treason!*

Not only that, but both of them are taking what belongs to the people and they are ruling the country by using the terror of their cut-throat bandit friends! I have been told by the current baron of the Exchequer that England is almost bankrupt due to the action of my mother and Roger Mortimer!"

He decided to await the arrival of some of his friends who were coming to Nottingham to attend the Parliament being held there in October. With them was Henry, the Earl of Lancaster. Soon after the arrival of Henry, he, and Edward III, held a long and earnest discussion.

Henry said, *"Your majesty, how are things going for you?"* Edward replied, *"Things are no-good, thank you Henry, but thank you for asking!"* Henry said, *"What are the problems or the problem?"* Edward III replied, *"My mother and Sir Roger Mortimer are ruling England as regents, but they do not have a commission from Parliament to do so! The are keeping me, the rightful king who was appointed as such by Parliament just after the removal of my father as King!*

Since my mother and bloody Mortimer started ruling, they have both greatly enriched themselves at the expense of other people! Not only that, but I have been directly asked by the Baron of the Exchequer to end the rule of both mother and Mortimer because the treasury only has less than £46 left in it! Please Henry, let me lend some of your soldiers so that I can lead them into the chamber where mother and Mortimer are both staying in Nottingham Castle and arrest both of them!"

Henry of Lancaster thought over what he had been told. He said, *"Your majesty, from what you have just told me, I can see that both your mother, Isabella and her lover, Sir Roger Mortimer are guilty of both theft and treason! Therefore, I am putting the thirty-man platoon of infantry soldiers with whom I arrived, at your disposal your majesty!"* Edward exclaimed, *"Excellent, Henry!"* With those words spoken, Henry led Edward to his platoon of thirty soldiers.

Henry the Earl of Lancaster addressed his soldiers while in the company of Edward. He said, *"Men, many of you have had or know of someone who has had their property forsaken by Queen Isabella and her lover called Sir Roger Mortimer!*

The man who you can see here in front of me is your true king! I have pleasure in introducing you all to King Edward III, who appointed as the King by Parliament when his father, Edward II was deposed! If you love England as I do, you shall immediately swear allegiance to him and go into action on his behalf! In an hour from now, I must give a speech in Parliament being held here in Nottingham! So, I order you to come forward and to pledge allegiance to King Edward III!"

So, it was that the thirty members of the private army of Henry the Earl of Lancaster came forward and pledged their allegiance directly to their king. Edward was delighted by that. He said, *"Thank you, Earl of Lancaster, and my loyal soldiers! We must move swiftly now! I know that both my mother and Sir Roger Mortimer are in her chambers at Nottingham Castle right now, and it's very likely that the two of them shall remain in my mother's chambers or the rest of the day! We should use this opportunity to arrest them both!"*

Having said that, he said, *"Gentlemen, it is time to draw your weapons and to arrest my mother and Mortimer for treason!"* A sergeant who was present said, *"Sir, if we were to move as a block by all of us moving against your mother and her lover, the alarm would very quickly spread all over Nottingham Castle and that could result in the wanted pair of people escaping! Your majesty, I know that it would be far better if we only use a ten-man section to arrest the two of them!"*

King Edward III said, *"Thank you, sergeant! I like your proposal and that is what shall happen! Sergeant, assign your best section and section commander the task of arresting Queen Isabella and Sir Roger Mortimer!* That was done, then Edward said, *"Men, we are now very near to the chambers of my mother and Sir Roger Mortimer!"*

The king, although he was only sixteen years of age, burst through the door of his mother's chambers in Nottingham Castle. As he was going through the doorway, he shouted *"Mother and Roger Mortimer, you are both under immediate arrest for treason!"* Mortimer tried to fight the approaching soldiers, but they quickly overpowered him, and he was made prisoner. Mortimer could not help himself! For some reason, he began to belittle the King.

He mockingly said, *"And now the high and mighty King Edward III wants all England to acknowledge him! Listen to me, Sir Roger Mortimer and you will see that the king is a mere boy who should still be under the supervision of his mother and me!"*

Edward was livid at the remarks of Mortimer. He said, *"Sir Roger Mortimer, You are guilty of high treason and larceny! I do not care how you may plead about this because you shall not have a trial, so ensuring that you cannot rely upon the use of smooth words and other tricks to get you out of the charges this time! Instead of a public trial, you shall be taken to the place of execution at Tyburn. There, you shall hang by your neck, until you are dead! That sentence has been passed against you and I have the warrant for your death. As I have said before, you shall be hanged by your neck until you ae dead, you low-grade traitor!"*

Mortimer, realising the fix that he was in, tried to bluff his way out of the problem. He said, *"So, Edward the Third, King of England, you appear to not understand the right of Englishmen to have a fair and open trial! That part of English law applies equally to surfs and nobles! Even to kings!"* Edward shouted, *"Sir Bloody Roger Mortimer! It is very apparent that you know little to nothing about English Law or French Law!*

It matters not what you think! The simple fact remains that I, Edward III, am the true King of England! As such, I am the law and don't you forget it! I have decreed that you shall hang without this ever going to trial! By your death at the end of a rope at Tyburn, you shall be put back into your place and you shall die like the surf that you really are! Now say no more or you shall be gagged and then taken to your place of execution at Tyburn! You shall hang by the neck until your death on the 30th of November!"

Meanwhile, Isabella was pleading with her son about Mortimer. She said, *"Good son, good son, have pity upon my gentle Mortimer!"* Edward responded with, *"Really Mother, do you really want me to show* pity towards this poor excuse for a man who is just a thief, liar, and coward? Don't you get it mother? This man killed my father, and he poisoned your mind to the point where you were also against my father, and you organised his downfall!

He has left many people destitute and in total poverty by taking their lands and giving it to himself and those in his direct employ! Remember how Mortimer had Edmund the Earl of Kent executed for attempting to rescue my father? The fact is that Mortimer started those rumours saying that Kent would rescue my father, when in fact that was nothing but lies! Mortimer took Kent's lands for himself as soon as Kent was killed!

That brings me to how he has managed to portray you as some sort of evil woman who is extremely greedy, and people are saying that your avarice is to blame to the excesses that were practised during the rule of yourself and Mortimer! Now hear me Mother, after the execution of Mortimer, you shall remain under guard. Eventually, you shall be released.

Then you shall live comfortably at Castle Rising in Norfolk as the Queen Dowager! I shall visit and you shall have complete freedom to travel, and you shall be given the respect normally given to a Queen Dowager! You shall lose some of your lands and income, but in return, you will be given everything that you enjoyed as the Queen Consort!

You shall be free to visit Windsor Castle as you see fit, and I shall welcome you when you do so! Now then Mother, I have much to do, and I cannot just be here talking to you all of the time! I have England to run efficiently and along a 'Ready for War' footing!' That is because England has enemies, and one of them appears to be from your former home of France!"

By informing his mother of his concerns about France, Edward III was in fact laying the groundwork for his long-held ambition. The attempted conquest of France by England and the beginning of the *"Hundred Years War!"*

Isabella as Dowager Queen

As he was betrothed to Philippa of Hainault from an early age, Edward welcomed being able to finally get married to her and to make her his lover. After checking possible dates for the royal wedding, Edward decided that the marriage would go ahead on the 24th of January in 1328. He was still very much the son of Isabella who relished her new role as the dowager queen. That was the reason for his calling out to his courtiers, *"Send scribes and messengers to me immediately!"*

That resulted in two scribes hurrying to Edward and when they reached him, they said, *"Your majesty, what is it that you want us to do?"* Edward replied, *"Scribes, it is now the 2nd of December 1327 and I need you to draft two copies of a letter to my mother, who is the dowager, Queen Isabella! You shall inform her that the marriage between myself and Philippa of Hainault shall take place on the 24th of January of 1328 and that the service shall take place at the cathedral called York Minster. Inform her that she is both invited to be there and that I wish to see her there for the occasion! She* shall have all of the courtesy and rights of a dowager queen and she must be afforded the utmost respect!"

The scribes left the immediate vicinity of the king and got to work drafting the two copies of the letter. Several days later, Isabella received the written invitation, and it thrilled her. Attending the marriage in York, she began thinking, *"Well Edward my Dear Heart, here I am at the wedding of our son Edward III and his bride of Philippa of Hainault! This wedding is truly a great sight to behold, and I am so happy that our son has chosen to invite me here for this great occasion! There was nothing that I could do to prevent Roger Mortimer from murdering you! At least our son has turned the tables on Mortimer, and both arrested and hanged him for what he did! I miss you, my love and when I die, I shall be placed into a grave next to you and I shall be wearing the clothing that I had on for our joint coronation. I will carry out the duties of dowager queen for our son and his children for as long as I live."*

The marriage between Edward III and Philippa of Hainault resulted in the birth of Prince Edward on the 15th of June 1330 at Woodstock Palace in Oxfordshire. Edward III informed Isabella of the birth and she hurried to be with her Grandson. Isabella asked, *"My good son, what shall be the name or names of your son?"* Edward III answered, *"Mother, I am glad that you have asked me that! He shall be named as Edward, after both myself as his father and his Grandfather before him! Due to the fact that he was born here at Woodstock Palace, people will call him Edward of*

Woodstock! So here you go, mother, hold your grandson and speak to him!"

That resulted in Isabella holding the baby and looking into his eyes. While she was looking into the child's eyes, she lost track of the fact that she was in the nursery of her son's family, and she began to dream. What she saw during her visions about the baby disturbed her and she spoke to her son Edward III about it.

She said, *"My good son, I have just seen a satisfying and also, disturbing vision of this baby boy! He shall become an outstanding warrior prince and many people shall call him the 'Black Prince' because of his love of black cloaks and black armour and shields! If you decide to invade France, he shall aid you considerably in action against the French and you shall make him the 'Prince of Wales' in 1343!*

Later, in 1346, you shall knight your son at La Hougue. I have seen that he shall become the very model of English knighthood and chivalry! On the down side of things, I have also seen that he shall die before he can come to the throne, and that his son called Richard shall become the king in his stead!"

With Edward III now firmly ruling as the King of England in his own right, and his mother *Isabella* was being set-up as the dowager queen, a role which she quickly grew to appreciate and embrace. Over time, Isabella increasingly found that she missed her family connection to the Royal House of France. (the French King Charles IV was her brother). So, when her son King Edward III of England wanted to speak to her about his own background within the French Royal Family, Isabella enthusiastically spoke to him about her French Royal Family background and explained how he fitted into the succession of the French King.

Speaking to Edward, Isabella said, *"Edward my good son, As far as I am concerned, when my brother Charles IV of France dies, you shall have a very strong claim to the French throne! After all, you are the Earl of Aquitaine, even though you must pledge allegiance to Charles IV, the current king of France! So, my good son. Always remember that when King Charles IV of France dies, you shall be the closest living male relative to him and that shall give you a strong claim to the French throne!*

My good son, I would very much like to see you as the king of both England and France! If that is to happen for you, then you must take what is yours by divine right! In order to get things rolling along for you in a smooth and orderly manner, it is necessary for you to enlist the aid of the church by writing directly to the Pope and imploring him to help you to take you French crown which is yours by divine right! The Pope is bound to help you achieve this because you are the closest male relative of Charles IV!"

Edward answered, *"Very Well mother! I shall do as you have advised me!"* With that, Edward called for his scribes. When they arrived, he said, *"Scribes, draft out a letter to 'His Holiness', the Pope! The letter to him is to implore him to preach in the abbeys and churches in both Italy and France, that I, Edward III, King of England have the divine right to the French*

Crown upon the death of King Charles IV of France! Also, point out that such an action will result in the union of England and France, the result of which can only be good for both countries and for the Church!

Now go to it and get the job completed! I need you to not just make the letter easily readable, you must also tastefully decorate the letter and make it appear very attractive! Today is Monday and I am giving you until late Friday night to produce two identical copies of the letter! One copy shall be retained here as a file, while the other copy is sent to the Pope by 'Safe Hand Despatch'."

So it was that King Edward III of England called for a group of five male volunteers to act as the messengers who were to deliver the letter from him to the Pope in person. During the times of the twentieth century and the twenty-first century, someone who delivered a message by *'Safe -Hand'* was often armed with a side-arm such as a pistol. During the times of Edward and Isabella, these messengers were simply armed with swords and daggers, if they were armed at all.

So, after having obtained the five men he needed to act as *'Safe-hand Messengers'*, Edward armed his men and told them of the importance of their mission! He said, "Men your mission of safely getting this written message into the hands of the Pope is Vital! Everything in the letter is highly confidential and no-one in the world other than the Pope is permitted to read it or any part of it! Any-one else in the world found to have read the letter shall become guilty of treason against both England and the Church! That offence is punishable by excommunication followed by death by hanging or other means as deemed to be suitable punishments by the crown of England and the Vatican!"

Edward III's Letter Delivered to the Pope

The group of five messengers set-off on their journey to the Vatican in Rome! A member of the Swiss Guard approach the Pope. He saluted him and said, *"Your Holiness, I have a group of messengers from King Edward III of England they have an important letter for you! They refuse to give the letter to anyone else but yourself! Apparently, that is what the English people call 'Safe-Hand Despatch'. Also, They have been told to wait until such time as you see fit to answer them by writing a return letter to Edward! What is your pleasure Your Holiness?*

The Pope answered, *"Lieutenant, you have done your job well! Tell the five Englishmen that I shall see them immediately! Also get at least three of my best scribes to draft out my reply letter to King Edward II of England!"* That having been said, the Lieutenant of the Swiss Guard informed the English messengers that the Pope would see them immediately.

As the messengers were escorted to the throne room of the Pope, they could see the Pope seated on his throne and that he was flanked by the scribes he had asked for. The messengers were under the command of Sir Humphries who now took command. He said, *"Your Holiness, I am Sir Humphries, my men and I are here to deliver unto you, a personnel letter from King Edward*

III to you! We have been ordered to remain here with you until you give us a reply letter for King Edward III!"

The pope took the letter and read it! He then said, *"Gentlemen, as soon as my scribes have finished writing out of my response to King Edward III of England, you shall take the one of the two copies to England to the King! One copy is for the king, while the other copy meant for use as a file copy, and it shall remain here! The information contained within the letter is for the eyes of King Edward III only and it is completely confidential! See to it that only King Edward III reads it! If anyone else to reads it, the person concerned shall be guilty of treason against both God and King Edward III! Anyone found guilty of treason against both God and the king of his country must die by being excommunicated and then hanged!"*

The Pope's Answer to Edward III's Letter

In reply to Edward III's letter, the Pope had written, *"Dear Edward III, My dearest son, You are the Grandson of King Charles IV of France and you have asked me to rule upon your claim to the Crown of France. It has come to my attention that you are also the legal lord of the Duchy of Aquitaine and the county of Ponthieu in France and that you are the last full male relative directly related to Charles IV the King of France.*

On those basis, I concur that you shall have a legal claim to the throne of France after the death of Charles IV! However, I urge you to not do anything hasty and to withhold all aggression in this matter! I believe that it will be far better to use diplomacy for you to get what you want.

I therefore urge you not to invade France if your claim to the French throne is rejected by the French princes after the death of Charles IV! I do support your claim the throne of France, but I need you to use peaceful means to take your objectives, for God wants all his children to resolve their differences peacefully!"

Signed Pope John XXII.

At Six Years, Prince Edward is called 'Black Prince'.

A courtier called Janet Smythe approached King Edward III. She said, *"Your majesty and my lord, Edward, I am Janet Smythe, and my duties are to cater for and to instruct your son Edward. The prince is currently only six years old, but already, he has shown that he is both fearless and that he likes to wear black clothing such as cloaks over his otherwise colourful clothing!*

According to your instructions, a suit of armour was completed for him at his current size. He rejected the armour, and told everyone in earshot, that he wants to only ever ware black armour!" The thought of his son asserting himself pleased King Edward III and he decided to back-up his son.

So, Edward III said, *"Now just think of what has happened here! You have been firmly told by my son, whom I now call the 'Black Prince', that normal armour shall not do and that he wants black armour! Now hear this! When you get a command from my son, you shall treat it as though the order has come from me! To disobey the 'Black Prince' shall be treated in the same way as disobeying my orders! Anyone found guilty of such action or actions shall be charged with treason and hanged! He has ordered you to obtain black armour of his size for him and you shall do it without complaint! Do I make myself clear?"*

Edward III Claims the French Throne

Feeling emboldened, King Edward III made a claim to the French throne as soon as news of the death of King Charles IV reached him. In July of 1337, a messenger arrived at Windsor Castle and demanded to immediately be brought before King Edward III! He said, *"I am Sir Antonio Doria, that means that I am the official English ambassador to France! I have urgent news for the ears of his Majesty, King Edward III, only! Now escort me into his presence or else lose your ugly heads!"* The receiving members of the household of Windsor Castle were unaccustomed to being spoken to in such a manner and so, their reaction was tardy to say the least!

The guard who was closest to Sir Antonio Doria when he came storming into Windsor Castle answered, *"Bullshit sir! The chief job of the guard of Windsor Castle is to safe-guard the King at all times! You cannot just barge into this royal place and begin to throw your weight around! All the same, I shall escort you to the King! Follow me!"* Finally, the ambassador and his escort were in the presence of King Edward III.

Edward thought that the antics of his guard were amusing, and he quickly dismissed him so that he could discuss whatever the problems were with France which were about to be told to him by the English ambassador to that place. So he said, *"Yes Sir Antonio Doria, what is the news from France and how do you think it shall affect me and my England?"*

The ambassador to France said, *"Your majesty, The King of France, called Charles IV has died. He has no direct male relatives and that means that you have a strong claim to the French Throne because Isabella, the sister of the French King Charles IV, is your mother. That in turn means that you and you alone, are the only surviving male who can be considered as a direct relative heir to the French Throne.*

However, your majesty, I must warn you that some men with lessor claims to the French throne are claiming it. Among these is the first cousin of Charles IV, called Phillip the Count of Valois! I have it on good authority that he shall be crowned King of France as King Phillip VI. Accordingly, I urge you to see that man and make him your ally! For only by so doing, can you avoid a possible conflict between England and France which is almost sure to happen otherwise!

Your majesty, you hold the French territory of Aquitaine and that forms a large part of the ancestral homeland of the English of Norman descent. The region of Gascony has been incorporated into Aquitaine. That region has its own language and customs. Red wine known as Claret is produced there and the region trades directly with England, which provides the English with much revenue! Your majesty, I urge you to consider the losses to England if you do not go to France and pledge allegiance to the new King Phillip VI of France. If you do not do so, he shall remove Aquitaine from English ownership and that shall prove to be very costly for England your majesty!"

That resulted in a stunned silence throughout the English court! After some time, King Edward III spoke again. He said, *"Very well ambassador! You have done very well in bring me these warnings of probable tensions with France over Aquitaine! Methinks that you are correct and that me must go to France and pledge allegiance to this new King Phillip VI of France as far as control of my French lands in Aquitaine are concerned! Therefore, by God and his mother, that is what shall happen!*

Scribes, prepare my letter of submission to the new King Phillip VI of France in all things to do with the control of Aquitaine and its regions. Let him know that I shall be in Paris to officially pay homage to him during what is left of year 1329!"

Provocations!

Although he had just made that statement, Edward did not like it at all, and he resolved to closely watch the French activities in case of treachery which he suspected the French of. He was right in not trusting the French because despite Edward's homage to Phillip, the French continued to interfere in Gascony. A messenger appeared at the throne room of Edward III.

He said, *"You majesty, there have been some skirmishes at some of the walled towns along the Gascon border! You may recall that an area of Gascony in French hands is known as Agenais and the French King Phillip VI has been contacting various lords of the region in order to take them away from English sovereignty and to recruit soldiers for use against England!*

Not only that, but I know that the French King wants to go on a crusade and that he has assembled a mighty fleet of ships! The main problem is that if Phillip decides to not crusade in the Holy Land, then that large fleet shall become a continuing threat to English existence, in particular if he moves it to ports along the French side of the English channel!"

Edward III replied, *"Messenger, you have done well in advising me of these things! Go to the royal Kitchen and both eat and drink your fill. You have done your duty and you are now excused!"* Just after that messenger had left, Sir Antonio Doria, again appeared before Edward III.

He said, *"Your majesty, your influential advisor called Robert III of Artois is in exile from France because he has fallen out with King Phillip VI because of an inheritance claim! The French King now says that unless you immediately extradite Robert III of Artois to France, that much great peril, and dissention shall occur for England."*

Things quickly went from being bad to much worse! The French King Phillip confiscated the English lands in Gascony which was immediately followed by Phillip seizing the county of Ponthieu. He called for the English ambassador to France! Upon the ambassador arriving King Phillip of France spoke.

He said, *"Ambassador from England, I have urgent work for you to complete on the behalf of both France and England! We need you to see King Edward III of England and make sure that he understands that we, the French nobility completely reject his assertion that he has more rights to the Crown of France than does the French King Phillip! See to it that he completely understands that France will fight England if he continues to make invalid claims upon the French Throne!*

See to it that he understands that the people of France reject his argument that that he is the only male directly related to the dead King Charles IV of France! That fact that his mother is the former French princess Isabella does not change anything at all. It must be remembered that she renounced her French citizenship when she became the wife of King Edward II of England, she also became burdened with English nationality and lost her French nationality! Furthermore, it does not matter what the Pope feels or thinks about the situation, because the English do not have any rights in France, and we shall fight the English to the death if they try to invade us!"

The Edwardian War

The early years of the of the one-hundred-year war became known as the Edwardian war because it was started by King Edward III, before the beginning of hostilities, the French King repeated his demands for the English to extradite Robert III of Artois to France, as expected by the French King, that was rejected by King Edward III of England. He called his ambassador to France into his court in order to confer with him about what was quickly becoming a prelude to war!

He said, *"Ambassador, it has come to my attention that the fucking French have become the allies of the Scots who have given England such a problem! I need you to go to Paris and inform the French upstart and illegal king that I, Edward III am the true King of England and France and that I shall invade France immediately if the French do not immediately end their objectionable alliance with the Scottish King! As well, the French must plead total allegiance to me as the true King of France!"*

The English ambassador to France, Sir Antonio Doria, answered with, *"What you are asking me to do, your majesty, sounds like you are declaring war! Is that your intent, your majesty?"* King Edward III of England answered, *"Yes! Now go to Paris with my ultimatum that the French shall immediately cease their alliance with King David II of Scotland and the French shall then appoint me as the King of France and England! Unless all of what I demand is done, a state of war shall be imposed upon France with immediate effect!"*

When King Phillip of France was told, he said, *"So, war is what the English vassals of Edward III want! I was always correct in never trusting the English! Therefore, war is what they shall have! Prepare to move the fleet which was meant to take me on crusade to the Holy Land to areas where it can be used to mount an invasion of England!"*

The English Invasion of France

During 1337, the English army commanded by King Edward III and his son, Prince Edward who was widely known as "The Black Prince" led the English armies on successful campaigns across France. The son of Edward III was also named as Edward and due to his love of black cloaks and black armour, he became known as *'The Black Prince'*. He was energetic and earned the distinction of being one of the best commanders of the English side during the early years of the One Hundred Years War. He was regarded as by his English comrades as being the epitome of chivalry and one of the greatest knights of his time.

During early 1337, King Edward III was speaking to his eldest son, Edward the 'Black Prince'. He said, *"Edward my son, in order to safe-guard our country of England from French aggression during our war with the French, I have just created the first dukedom in England! You shall become the Duke of Cornwall by the middle of next year (1338) and as such, you be the guardian of the kingdom of England, and you shall govern the country whenever I have to be absent due to my commitment of fighting the French* forces! How do you feel about that awesome responsibility my son?"

The 'Black Prince' Becomes Duke of Cornwall

The son of King Edward III was most impressed by what his father was saying. He replied, *"Methinks that it is wonderful that you, my father has such a great confidence in me that you are giving me the honour of ruling England on your behalf whenever you must be away from here! Thank you, my father for giving me this great opportunity to prove myself in the eyes of yourself and the people of England! I shall be the best knight that England has ever produced and also, I shall be the best commander on the English side!"*

Listening to what his son had told him, filled King Edward III with a great joy, for he knew that his son would quickly do exactly what he had just said. The King said to the Black Prince, *"Edward my son, you have done well, and I am publicly making you the 'Prince of Wales' during this year of 1343. That will ensure your succession to my throne! Your Grandmother Isabella shall be present during this great moment!"*

During July of 1346, King Edward III spoke to his son, Edward the 'Black Prince'. He said, *"My son, the time has come for us both to depart England and travel to our ancestral home in Normandy. Soon after we arrive there, I shall knight you at the cathedral of La Hougue in public. Be sure to wear your black armour on that auspicious occasion.*

Your Grandmother, the dowager Queen Isabella, will be in attendance at the ceremony. I am sure that it will bring her a great joy! The main reason that I want you to wear your black armour is that you are already well known as the 'Black Prince'. The sight of me knighting you while you are dressed in your black armour shall very quickly be known all over France and that shall give us a propaganda victory!"

So, King Edward III knighted his eldest son, the 'Black Prince' at La Hougue and the news spread like a wild-fire all over Europe and even the French court knew about it! Isabella attended the ceremony, and it made her happy. During the ceremony King Edward III drew his sword and gently touched his son on both shoulders.

Having done so, he said, *"Arise, Sir Edward, knight of the garter and the Duke of Cornwall. Most people know you as the* 'Black Prince' *because of your love for black clothing and armour. We shall use that name to the advantage of Englishmen in our dealings with the French!"* As part of the ceremony of Knighthood, King Edward III announced a special appointment for the 'Black Prince'. King Edward III again spoke to Edward his son, 'Edward the Black Prince'.

He said, *"Edward my son, I am appointing you to the role of the* King's Lieutenant *when we reach Gascony. Once there, you shall lead an army into Aquitaine on a mission of 'Seek out the enemy everywhere in Aquitaine and destroy him using a series of raids'! We must keep the French wary and frightened* of English soldiers because by so doing we shall considerably weaken the French resistance to us! I have already made my name in military adventures by closing with and beating the Scottish army at the Battle of Bannockburn! Now, my son, it is high time for you to make your name in military action against our French enemies! I am sure that your reputation as the "Black Prince" shall aid the cause of England immeasurably!"

English Action at Crecy

Just a few days before the knighthood of the 'Black Prince' at La Hougue, King Edward III was in discussion with his son. He said, *"Edward, my son, I shall knight you as soon as we land at La Hougue! The service shall take place at the church known as Quettehou. After that, when the word spreads around the French army units that the famous Black Prince is leading tough soldiers against French army units, you must make a right good beginning by breaking through the Cotentin, burning, and pillaging as you and your army go!*

I need you to follow that up with distinguishing yourself at Caen where you have to close with and defeat the French forces under the command of the French Sir Godemar I du Fay, who shall try to stop you from crossing the Somme using the ford of Blanchetaque! See to it that you win, and conversely, that the French lose their positions and territory between our English army and the rest of Normandy!"

At first light of Saturday, the 26th of August 1346, Edward the Black Prince, and the Prince of Wales, received the sacrament from his father at Crecy.

King Edward III said to the Black Prince, *"My son, I have assigned the earls of Warwick, Sir Geoffroy d'Harcourt and the Earl of Oxford, Sir John Chandos, and other officers to your command to help you win against the French!*

As well as those leaders, you have eight hundred English men at arms, two thousand archers and one thousand Welsh infantry soldiers. Use your bowmen to cause havoc among the French and put their frontlines into disorder! When that happens disrupt the French second line using archers armed with English longbows! Be on the look-out for unexpected French reinforcing units coming to the aid of their second line!"

Meanwhile, the French Count of Alencon charged the positions of the Black Prince with great fury! The earls working with the Black Prince sent a message to King Edward III, saying that his son was in great danger. However, King Edward III responded to the pleas for help from the earls assisting his son by saying, *"I note that my son has not yet been wounded! I also note that he should have the glory that shall be his for defeating the French enemy!"*

While the King was speaking to his subordinates, the Black Prince was thrown off his horse and was in dire straits before he was rescued by his standard bearer, Sir Richard Fitzsimon, who threw down the banner and then stood over the body of the Black Prince beating back the French enemies while Edward the Black Prince regained his feet and was again a fearsome warrior. Harcourt now sent the Earl of

Arundel to help. As a result, the English forced back the French who were trying to gain some English held high ground.

Meanwhile, the French tried a flanking attack upon the English lines on the side of Wadicourt commanded by the Counts of Alencon and Ponthieu, however, the English held their lines and were strongly entrenched there. Resulting in both front lines being utterly broken and then the division of the French King Phillip was engaged. That now brought the Black Prince into direct conflict again and the French lost the Duke of Lorraine and the Counts of Alencon and Blois.

With the French forces in confusion and retreat, King Edward III appeared at the front of his vanguard and the rout of the French forces was complete! King Edward met his son and declared that his son had acquitted himself greatly. Next, the king embraced his son and the prince bowed low in order to pay homage to his father. On the following day, both men paid funeral honours to King John of Bohemia whom they had killed in action. The next action for the Black Prince was the siege of Calais during 1346 – 1347).

Siege of Calais

Ever since William the Conqueror became King William I of England, the Norman English aristocracy held land in Normandy which was a part of France. By the English monarchs having property in France, they had to become subservient to the French kings, becoming vassals of the French with regards to property they owned in France.

So it was that the French King Phillip VI, had serious disagreements with King Edward III of England regarding English ownership of properties in Normandy and others areas of France. On the 24th of May 1337, Phillip was present at the *'Great Council'* held in Paris. The leader of the elder statesmen present spoke, Eugene said, *"Your majesty, King Phillip, we the elder statesmen of France are concerned about the continuing English ownership of land in Normandy and other areas! If the English King Edward III and all other English lords who are land-owners in France do not swear allegiance to you, then we, the nobility of France must confiscate all land owned by the foreigners!"*

King Phillip replied, *"Yes Eugene, I see the problem, and I agree that all English lords owning property in France must come to France and swear allegiance directly to me in all matters to do with their French lands. Scribes, I order you to draft two copies of a letter to King Edward III of England. In it you are to inform him that unless he and other English Lords with property in France, they must come to Paris by the fifteenth of next month and in public, swear allegiance to me in all things to do with the French property that they own, or else, they shall all be in breach their obligations as vassals of France! The best copy of the letter is to be sent to King Edward III of England, while the second copy of the letter shall be kept in my library in Paris for future reference if it is needed!"* That resulted in the One Hundred Year war which actually lasted for one hundred and sixteen years.

The major French port on the side of the English channel was Calais which was ideally suited for the needs of Edward and his English armies. Calais was highly defensible it was surrounded by double moat, and it had formidable city walls. Calais also had a citadel located in its north-west corner which had its own moat and additional fortifications. Calais could be easily resupplied by sea as well as being easy to defend on land. King Edward III, spoke to his officers at an orders group on the 18th of July at Crecy.

He said, *"Gentlemen, before us lies the French port that we must take so that English resupplies and reinforcements can have a secure entry into France on our behalf! As you already know, we defeated the French army at Crecy where the French lost many of their soldiers! Also, French morale is at a very low ebb, and we must take advantage of the situation! For all of those reasons, England shall lay siege to Calais as of now and I expect the French to sue for peace in early August of next year (1347), because the French people there shall be starving by then!"*

As a result, Edward and his forces laid siege to Calais on the 3rd of September 1346. King Philip of France could not relive the city resulting in its starving defenders surrendering the 3rd of August 1347. That made Calais the only city to have been successfully besieged and starved into submission.

Amerigo of Pavia

The English possession of Calais allowed the English to accumulate supplies and materials which were needed for more campaigns against the French enemy. The city had a strong garrison of one thousand and two hundred (1,200) men. They were under the command of the Captain of Calais. He had many deputies and under-officers. One of them was Amerigo of Pavia.

Amerigo of Pavia served as the galley master of Calais as of April 1348. That also gave him command of a tower overlooking the Calais Harbour and an entrance into the citadel.

Geoffrey de Charny

The commander of the French forces near Calais in 1350 was Geoffrey de Chanry. Both he and his army tried to take Calais using trickery and subterfuge. At an orders group he was holding with his officers, he said, *"Gentlemen, it has unfortunately come to my attention that the English forces although smaller in number than the French forces are giving France a considerable hard time! I need you to come up with some ideas of how we can turn around the English advantage over us!"*

No-one spoke, and Geoffrey de Chanry realised that he would have to find the way of taking Calais off the English forces himself. After sometime, he again spoke to his officers, He said, *"Considering the important of Calais to Normandy and France in general, and how our forces appear to be inferior to the English army, I need some volunteers to go to Calais and to speak to Amerigo of Pavia. He is an Italian officer of the Calais City Garrison. By fair means or foul ones, you must get him to leave Calais and make sure that you bring him here to meet me in person!"*

He had just finished speaking when he was rudely interrupted by a junior officer. The young knight said, *"Sir, please allow me to remind you that not only do the English forces hold most territory in this part of France, but there is in existence, a truce between the English and French forces! It sounds to me sir, that you are planning on breaking the truce and using other sneaky underhanded tactics to obtain the things which you cannot get through fighting! Sir, I beg you to reconsider and not use subterfuge and trickery, use good old-fashioned honour and force-of-arms to get what France needs!"*

Geoffery de Charny replied, *"You sir, are a junior officer at best! Honour does not matter! Winning is all that matters! So, I repeat, I want some volunteers to go into Calais and see the Italian Officer of that city who has the name of Amerigo Pavia I need you to bring him here, so that I can bribe him to open the Calais City gates and let in our French forces!"*

So later that afternoon, a delegation from the French forces went to Calais under a flag of truce and arranged to see the Italian officer. After more time had elapsed, he was finally brought before the commander of French delegation.

Feeling somewhat indignant, Amerigo of Pavia spoke to the Frenchmen. He said, *"What in the name of God, do you Frenchmen want?"* The delegation of French knights said, *"We have been sent by the French commander called Geoffery de Charny to speak directly to you! He wants us to bring you back to his encampment when he shall make you an offer which* only a crazy man could refuse! So, sir, will you go with us to the encampment of the French forces? The offer of Charny is genuine!"* The Italian officer of Calais agreed to accompany the Frenchmen and they left for the French camp.

Arriving at the encampment of Geoffrey de Charny, Amerigo of Pavia was escorted to Charny. Seeing him coming, Charny said, *"Hail to you, Amerigo of Pavia! I have an offer of money for you that will set-up you and your son for life! I have on hand 20,000 écus (approximately £4,000,000 in A.D. 2022 terms)! Just think what you and your son can do with such an amount of money!"* The Italian officer said, *"Charny, that is an impressive and great amount of money! What do you want in exchange for it?"* Charny replied, *"Nothing major, I just want you to open the gate to the citadel of Calais and leave the gate open for my forces to enter the citadel. Once we do that, we shall kill all of the English occupiers of the city!"*

Meanwhile, Amerigo of Pavia was thinking, but he remained silent. He was thinking, *"Oh you arrogant French arsehole! You shall not get what you want from me! As soon as I have your money, I shall take it with me to King Edward III of England! I shall inform him of your plot and help him to conduct counter measures to what you are trying to do!"*

Informing Edward III

Amerigo went to Havering, which is near London to speak to the English King. After he had been escorted into the presence of King Edward III during the afternoon of the 23rd of December 1349, Amerigo of

Pavia spoke. He said, *"Your majesty, I have been offered the sum of 20,000 écus by the French Commander of forces in this area if I open the gates to the citadel of Calais for him and his army!"*

King Edward replied, *"Thank you, Amerigo for this timely warning! Because of the fact that you have come to me out of your own free will to inform me of the great peril that is being organised against me, I shall forgive you and you shall become part of my counter-plan against Charny and his French morons! As to the money that you shall be paid by Charny, I shall keep three quarters of it for use against the French. Do not despair about this, because if you had not come to me like this, I would have had no option but to sentence you to be hanged, drawn, and quartered!*

That means you would have been hanged, but not long enough to kill you, then you would have been stretched on the rack until your bones broke, after that you would have been disembowelled, followed by your body being chopped into four pieces which then would have been buried in four separate locations at least eighty miles from each other and the places where the parts of your body are buried would remain a secret!

You are for now, excused and I shall speak to you again, regarding your role in the bringing down of the French Commander Geoffrey de Charny! Kindly remember that I hold your brother in order to make sure that you obey me! That is all for today, we shall continue this discussion tomorrow, the 24th of December at midday!"

At their next meeting one day later, King Edward III was then silent for a short time, after which he spoke. He said, *"So Amerigo, I now want you to tell me all that you know about the enemy commander called Geoffrey de Charny!"* Amerigo said, *"Geoffrey de Charny is a senior and well-respected Burgundian knight in the service of France! In 1346, he had just returned from a crusade in the Holy Land when he was called upon to assist his king's son during his campaign in the south of France.*

During 1347, he was leading the French army when it approached Calais in order to relieve the French garrison there. As the French approached the city, they found that the English were too well entrenched there and because the English presence was such a strong one it would be suicidal attack them! Therefore, King Phillip of France ordered that Charny attack your son, the Black Prince by challenging him to bring his army out into the open field and to then fight Carny and his men! As you know, your majesty, the Black Prince accepted the challenge with the result of a devastating loss of the French forces! I know that is the reason Charny tried to bribe me to open the city gate at the citadel!"

King Edward replied, *"Today is the 24th of December and I have nine hundred men. These are made up of three hundred man-at arms and six hundred archers armed with English longbows! Amerigo, remember that I am holding your brother and if you step outline in any way, first, he shall die, and he will be followed by you! So, do your duty to me and my England and all shall be well! In order to maintain secrecy, the expeditionary force shall be under the command of Sir Walter Manny, who was the previous First Captain of Calais! Serve me well, Amerigo, you have a limited command, and remember that I am holding your brother!"*

French Preparations

Meanwhile, Charny assembled a force of five thousand and five hundred soldiers at Saint-Omer, located twenty-five miles (forty kilometres) from Calais. The commanders of the force included most of the senior ranking soldiers of the French army. Opposing them were the one thousand and two hundred soldiers of the Calais garrison and several hundred English inhabitants living within the local area who could be called upon to aid the English forces opposing their French enemies.

Charny realised that the French needed a strong force which could not be repulsed by the strong garrison defending Calais. The gate controlled by Amerigo proved to be very difficult to approach by the large number of soldiers making up Charny's forces. The purpose of the gate was to provide an easy access to the Harbour for the crews of ships anchoured there. There were many approach problems for any invading force.

The gate could only be reached by men going towards it on foot, only at low tide and along a narrow beach right up to the city walls. The progress an invading force also had difficulty in that Calais was within a broad belt of marshes. The only roads through them were controlled by English Blockhouses.

Feeling frustrated by the defences of Calais, Charny turned to problem of enemy occupation of Calais over to his sub-ordinates. He said, *"Look here all of you who are in the service of France! We have a severe problem in that the English enemy and their vassals are holding Calais! The defence of Calais was already strong because of its strong garrison.*

As well, we must come up with a way of by-passing the English blockhouses and taking Calais. Well, do not just stand there doing nothing! It is critical for French forces to come up with a workable plan to beat the English and their vassals who holding Calais!"

After a few moments silence, a young French knight spoke. He said, *"Sir, you already have appealed to the greed of the Italian keeper of the gate of the citadel of Calais. You have successfully bribed him to leave the gate open for your forces!*

Just leaving that aside for a moment, I suggest that we wait until the night of the 31st of December when darkness is at its maximum and low tide would be shortly before dawn. I think that the English sentries will be either drunk from celebrating the coming of the new year or that they may be asleep.

That will allow us to bypass the blockhouses and our main force could reach Calais before dawn. With the main part of our French army waiting not far from Calais, a small force of one hundred and twelve men could enter the citadel. Some of our men could secure the citadel for us while others make their way through the sleeping city and go towards the Boulogne Gate and open it for us. The gatehouse would then be seized by us and the main gate to the city opened, allowing our entire army into Calais! Led by cavalry and other soldiers, our forces can enter and wipe out the citadel defenders!"

Pleased by the possibility of a break-through as suggested by the young knight, Charny replied, *"A well-thought-out solution to the problem Sir Knight! I like it! Now, does anyone have any questions about this?"*

Again, the knight answered, *"Sir, as I am about to engage the enemy in battle, I would like to know which of their commanders I shall be facing! Can you tell us that sir, or do we not know?"* Charny said, *"I know with certainty that we are facing at least the Earl of Suffolk, Lord Montagu, Lord Stafford, Lord Beauchamp, Lord Berkeley, and Lord de la Warr. Presently. I do not know if King Edward or his son, the Black Prince will be in action against us or not!"*

Battle for Calais

During the evening of the 31st of December 1349, Charny went to the head of his forces and took command. In front of his soldiers, he said, *"This glorious evening we shall liberate Calais from the strange people from across the English Channel! I have been able to bribe the Italian keeper of the gatehouse to the citadel to leave the citadel gate open for us and even to help to wipe out the small one hundred- and twelve-man detachment which shall carry out our operations at the citadel! While the citadel is being attacked by our small detachment, the main force shall bypass the English blockhouses and attack the*

Boulogne Gate. French soldiers of both the main force and the detachment attacking the citadel, to your duties, fall out!" Upon hearing that, the French soldiers did split into the two groups and go to their assigned positions.

The Attack of the Citadel Detachment

Shortly before dawn and while it was still dark, the advance party of the Citadel detachment approached Amerigo's gate-tower. The French soldiers were pleasantly surprised to that the gate to the citadel was indeed open, and that Amerigo was waiting to greet them in person. As the French detachment approached him, Amerigo said, *"Welcome to my area of responsibility for the citadel of Calais! Come with me and I shall lead you to where you need to be!"*

That resulted in Amerigo leading three French knights and their men-at-arms into the gate-house itself! Shortly after that, the French standard was flying over the top of the gate-house tower. That was seen by the remaining French soldiers of the citadel detachment and so, more Frenchmen crossed the drawbridge over the moat. Next a loud voice yelled in English, *"Select your targets and kill the French!"*

That was yelled as the drawbridge was raised and the portcullis was lowered. To their horror, the French invaders of the English positions saw that there were now sixty English men-at-arms running towards them with weapons raised and blood on their minds. The Frenchmen quickly surrendered resulting in all of the French who had entered the gate-house being captured.

Main Force at Boulogne Gate of Calais

Meanwhile, King Edward III of England, was waiting near the Boulogne Gate in plain armour with his household soldiers and a detachment of archers. At the sound of a trumpet, he led his forces through the opening gate and attacked the French under the banner of Walter Manny.

Surprised at the ferocity of the English attack upon them, and seeing many dead Frenchmen because of the English archers, the loud complaint of *"We have been betrayed"*, echoed around the French positions. With that, a large part of Charny's army fled! That caused Charny to hastily re-organise his remaining soldiers. King Edward III saw that things were becoming difficult for the French and that the progress of their army had slowed down markedly.

He spoke to his messenger saying, *"Go to the area of the North Gate and find my son, the Black Prince! When you see him, you must give him this message from me. 'My son, you must immediately lead you own household knights out of the North Gate, the Water Gate and proceed along the beach, past the citadel and then close with and kill the French army's exposed left flank!"*

So it was that the Black Prince hurried to aid his father in fighting the French. As the fighting of army of the English King and the French progressed, members of the English garrison of the Calais citadel quickly re-armed themselves and joined the fight against the French forces of Charny. Loud cheers were heard from the English army as its members saw the arrival of the garrison of Calais. With the arrival of the garrison from Calais, came renewed fighting of bitter intensity. Suddenly, there was once again loud cheering from the English side. That was because of the arrival of the Black Prince and his nine hundred men.

Although things were now much better for the English forces, the fact remains that Charny forces still outnumbered the English! At the sound of the trumpets of the Black Prince, and the sight of his nine hundred men approaching the French positions, the French army members broke and ran from the battlefield as fast as they could. Over two hundred French men-at-arms were killed in action (KIA). Thirty French knights were taken prisoner. Among the French prisoners was Charny, who now had a serious head wound. Also captured with Charny were Eustace de Ribeaumont and Oudart de Renti, while Pépin de Wierre was killed.

Events After the Battle for Calais

If the knights of European armies became prisoners during the 14th century, they became the personal property of their captors. King Edward III having fought in the front ranks, therefore claimed many of the French prisoners as his own. Among those French knights he claimed as his prisoners was the French leader, Charny.

That evening, King Edward III, had Charny and his higher-ranking officers dine with the English King. When they were all seated and dining, Edward III, spoke to Charny. He said, *"Look here Charny, I was always fighting you French incognito so that none of you lot would recognise me! That has worked well, and you are now my prisoners of war!*

So, Charny, what am I supposed to do with you? I shall set a ransom for you at an annual gratuity of one hundred marks! (about £80,000 in terms of 2023). *I do not understand why you, Charny, abandoned your chivalric values by both by fighting during a truce and by your dishonest way of attempting to purchase your way into Calais rather than to fight for it!"*

The facts about Charny are that he was considered to be a paragon of knightly virtue and honour. He was hailed by his contemporaries a true and perfect knight. Therefore, the insults and barbs from the English King were to strike deep blows during the active propaganda war between England and France.

Ribeaumont was quickly released on parole, so that word would be taken back to King Phillip of France about the French debacle at Calais. He later voluntarily travelled to England and surrendered himself until his ransom was paid. Many of the prisoners-of-war were released after they had promised not to fight against English forces until after they had redeemed themselves. Charny had to wait eighteen months for his release, because of the time it took to pay his ransom in full.

During the later months of 1350, The Grand Constable of France, and the Count of Eu, called Raoul, returned to France after spending over four years in English captivity. King Edward III was speaking to him. He said, *"Raoul, you have acquitted yourself honourably during my fights with the French forces. I am releasing you prior to the hand-over of your ransom which has been set at eighty thousand écus. Your subordinates shall be given more time to pay."* At the time, that was a common method of settling ransoms.

The French King, John II was dismayed that the English were still in full control of Calais and needing to put the blame upon someone else for the continued English occupation of Calais, he chose have Raoul executed for treason, when in fact he was a loyal French soldier of ability! So, the actions of the French King caused an uproar in France because of the French Crown's interference with a nobleman of high status. The English forces made full use of that to spread their propaganda campaigns against the French enemy.

On the 3rd of January 1352, Sir Walter Goines of the English side was in conversation several other free-lancing English soldiers who were on the lookout for opportunities to enrich themselves. Walter Goines said, *"My dear fellow English soldiers, before us, is the extremely strong French position of Guines, which is currently proving to be a thorn in the side of our English forces!*

We have been observing the activity of the French there, and we have noted that they have regular changes of men posted as sentries in Guines. I propose that we wait until about half-way through the change of sentry shift before we attempt to storm Guines during the middle of the night! By doing so, we shall only be facing the bored and half-asleep sentries and we should be able to take the position by using 'Escalade' as our means of attack.

For those of you English soldiers who do not know what 'Escalade' means, it consists of a group of attacking soldiers advancing to the base of a wall and then setting up a series of ladders and climbing up them to engage their enemies on top of the fortification walls! It is a most simple and direct way of engaging the enemy.

It is dangerous to be sure, but it is also simple and effective! We continue to observe the French and assuming all things remain as they now are, we shall launch our attack upon the base of the walls of the citadel one hour after the change of sentries! Now, maintain and clean your weapons and rest, Be ready for immediate action against the French defenders of Guines during the middle of the night on the 5th of January! Dismiss until you are required for action!"

So, during the middle of the night, the English practice of quietly observing the French paid off! The French sentries were changed, and the English waited for one hour, knowing that the defenders would soon be bored and inattentive. After that, the English group of soldiers silently began their escalade of placing their five long ladders against the wall. They then climbed up the ladders. It was a very dark night without any moonlight at all.

Sir Walter Goines led his men along the top of the wall of Guines after they had climbed up their ladders against the wall. As the group of English soldiers continued along the top of the walls, they encountered a French sentry who was asleep! In order to maintain the impetus of the attack on Guines, the

English soldiers cut the throat of the sentry and continued their attack.

Things continued to be done along these lines until the English soldiers decided to come off the wall and go into the French barracks. Soon after arriving there, the English quietly and efficiently took the French position after killing the sleeping French soldiers in their beds.

Walter Goines spoke to his men. He said, *"Gentlemen, you have all excelled yourselves! The French citadel of Guines is now ours! I thank you deeply for the way you have ensured yet another total English victory against the French enemy!"* Meanwhile, the French were furious! When news of the fall of the French citadel at Guines was brought to the attention of the French, they arrested their own acting commander and charged him with treason and dereliction of duty. Next, he was hanged, drawn, and quartered.

At the same time, the French sent a strong protest to King Edward III about it. Edward was therefore placed into a difficult situation because of a breach of a truce. For England to keep Guines meant a loss of honour and the immediate resumption of warfare, for which Edward was unprepared. He therefore ordered the English occupiers to hand it back to the French.

Financing the English Attack

During the following week, the English Parliament was scheduled to assemble. With several different members of the *Kings Council* making fiery war-mongering speeches in Parliament the English Parliament approved three years of war taxes. That caused Edward III to change his mind and by the end of January, he called for his messengers.

After they had arrived, Edward gave them their orders. He said, *"Messengers, I am sending you to Calais with important new orders for the English garrisons there and at other places including Guines! I want the messages delivered directly to the Captain of Calais and his sub-ordinate at Guines! You shall travel to Calais and Guines in two teams of three men. You shall all be armed, but you are to avoid contact with the enemy!*

Your mission is to take my written orders to the English commanders in Calais and Guines. The orders are in three sealed water-proof containers.

Anyone who opens these containers who is not an English knight in the service of my army forces stationed at Calais or Guines shall be considered to be an enemy of England and dealt with accordingly! Now take the sealed containers and leave on your mission!"

The teams of messengers did as they were asked to, and they delivered the King's orders at Calais and Guines. A direct result of that was the Captain of Calais taking over the garrison at Guines in the name of King Edward III of England. Thus, the war resumed. As part of the orders, the English had been strengthening the defences of Calais. That included the construction of fortified towers located at bottlenecks on roads through the marshes to the city.

Amerigo Returns to Service with the English

Now that war had resumed between England and France, Amerigo returned to service with the English forces. The English Captain of Calais spoke when Amerigo was sent to see him. He said, *"Amerigo, you have proven your loyalty to England as far as I am concerned! Although some of the staff of the English headquarters do not like you at all, I am giving you a new command. I am posting you to command the new tower at Fretun, located three miles (4.8 km) to the south-west of Calais! How do you like the idea of your new position?"*

Amerigo in fact did not like what he was hearing at all. He said, *"Sir, I do not understand! You have welcomed me back to English command, but you have told me that I am not really trusted by the English high command in spite of the fact that I was instrumental in the English Victory when the French tried to take the Calais citadel!*

Instead of rewarding me for letting King Edward of England know about the plot by the French commander Charny for me to open the citadel gate for the French, I feel that you are in fact downgrading my standing! Very well then, I shall do as you ask and go the tower at Fretun!"

Charny Again Commands French in the North East

The main fighting was against Guines. Geoffrey de Charny during 1352, had again been put in command of all French forces in the north east of France. The English garrison at Guines had one hundred and fifteen soldiers. Charny brimming with confidence, bragged to his men. He said, *"Hear me, fellow French soldiers! Today we shall get revenge upon the English for driving us out of Guines, because we shall retake the town!"*

The reason for his confidence was that his army had a strength of four thousand and five hundred men. So it was that he re-occupied the town after much fighting. Although his forces had taken the town, the possession of its keep was another matter! In spite of repeated attacks against the English whom he considered to be inferior soldiers, his large army could not take the keep and it remained a thorn in his side!

Then, in July, during the middle of the night, came the sounds of men yelling and cursing. Charny demanded to know what all the noise was about, and he did not like it when he was told by one of his knights. The knight said, *"Sir the noise that you can hear is being made by an English attack upon our sleeping French soldiers. Apparently, the Black Prince ordered that the English Garrison at Calais launch a surprise attack upon our positions here at Guines and the flames that you can see are your siege weapons and other war machines being burnt by the English forces, sir!"*

The news that his soldiers were being killed when they had taken an English held town frustrated Charny. He said, *"By God and his mother! Those English mad-men scare the shit out of me! As of now, we shall abandon this siege and we shall march to Fretun where we shall launch a surprise night-time attack against my old enemy Amerigo and his men! I have special plans in mind for Amerigo and the likes of him!"*

Arriving at the Fretun while it was still dark, during the night of the 24th of July, Charny and his forces launched their surprise night attack of the tower. Seeing that they were under attack by the entire French army, the garrison commanded by Amerigo howled in dismay and then fled, leaving the tower and its contents unguarded.

Leading another attack upon the tower was a knight from Normandy called Gene Montford. He was at the head of his detachment of men-at-arms when they burst through a bedroom door at top of the tower. Located at the top of the tower was the bedroom of Amerigo and his mistress. After bursting through the door, the French soldiers could see Amerigo and his English mistress.

Seeing Amerigo, the knight yelled out, *"Amerigo, I am arresting you for treason against France in the name of King John II of France! Get dressed and come quietly!"* Amerigo got dressed and was escorted to Charny. He smiled and said, *"Amerigo, I am happy to finally have you where I want you! In the morning we shall all journey to Saint-Omer where I shall disband my troops. While we are at Saint-Omer, you Amerigo shall be the be the prize exhibit! Before my soldiers depart, they and the population from miles around shall be gathered and they will all witness you being tortured to death.*

You shall have red-hot iron poked into your eyes after your fingers and toes have been chopped off and thrown upon a fire in front of you and close to you. I personally would like it if your penis was served and you were castrated with your genitals also being thrown upon the fire, but I have been overruled in that. You shall beg for death to be released your from your pain!

You can have the satisfaction of knowing that by your suffering, I am getting my revenge! As to your remains, your body shall be chopped into quarters and then the parts of it will be disposed of at four different locations a long way from each other!" These sorts of things were common place all over Europe during the 14th century. It had nothing to do with one nationality being any worse than a different one!

Chivalry and National Identity

As of the year 1337, King Edward III became the bastion and promoter of English chivalry and knighthood. He decided to set an example of how Royal Behaviour would benefit others in England and set about becoming the very embodiment of English chivalry and knighthood.

Edward and his court were in Calais, France, in 1358, where they were all attending a ball during the 'Feast of the Garter'. Also present at the ball was the female favourite of Edward, called Joan of Kent. During the festivities, she slipped and that caused her to drop her garter, which resulted in many others present at the ball ridiculing her and that caused her a great deal of embarrassment and distress. People were openly criticising her for having dropped her garter both to her face and behind her back. That caused her to be greatly embarrassed!

King Edward III was also present at the ball, and when the other guests at the function began to assemble in groups of people who were against Joan of Kent, He rectified the situation for her. Seeing that she was in distress, Edward went to her aid and silenced the assembled guests. He did so by picking up her garter and then he tied it to his knee.

He then yelled at the guests, *"I am disgusted by the behaviour of the guests at this ball! Too Many of you are passing bad judgement upon a lady who has had the misfortune of her garter working loose and then falling to the floor! I am instituting a new honour award called 'Order of the Garter'. It shall be awarded to deserving people of distinction who perform great services to our country of England!"*

Events and speeches such as that by Edward, as well as the war with France combined to form a stronger sense of national identity for the English people. As well, the war with both Scotland and France along with feeling of unease about possible invasions from either place united the aristocracy and that also led to the common people having a sense of belonging to England as well as accepting the English-Norman aristocracy.

Meanwhile, Edward took full advantage of the fears of the English people and decided to revive the English language. That resulted in him introducing *'The Statute of Pleading'* which ordered that only the

English language could be used in all English Courts of Law.

It the following year of 1363, Edward opened Parliament and for the first time, all debates and official announcements were in the English language. With English now being used in law courts and for the opening and running of Parliament, it also resulted in English literature flowering. That resulted in the works of William Langland, *"The Canterbury Tales"* by Geoffery Chaucer and the works of John Gower becoming popular, resulting the English language having a revival.

Meanwhile, King Edward III's mother, the Dowager Queen Isabella was living at Hertford Castle, but she was in ill health. She had been the Queen of England, a Princess of France, and she had invaded England from France to depose her husband, Edward II and install their son, Edward III, onto the throne in his stead.

While she was alive, she had the satisfaction of making her own enemies suffer and of watching her son, Edward III, become one of the most illustrious kings of England. She also had the pride of seeing her grandson become famous as the Black Prince and she noted that he was considered to be the epitome of English knighthood She died in 1358, after seeing her son introduce the "Order of the Garter".

Cheshire Expedition

During 1353, there were disturbances occurring within the localities of Cheshire. Edward, the Black

Prince had been appointed as the 'Earl of Chester' and soon after his return to England, he was riding in the fields near his castle when a mounted messenger from his father, King Edward III, was seen to be riding towards him.

Being used to adverse situations in war, the Black Prine was suspicious of any approaching rider, and he ordered his escort to cover the approaching rider using their English longbows. However, the rider did nothing to further suspicion of him and everyone relaxed when the rider raised his visor in the action which came to be called a salute.

Having raised the visor of his helmet, Sir Harrow spoke. He said, *"Your Majesty, I am Sir Harrow, and I am the main messenger of your father, King Edward III. He has ordered that I inform you, the Black Prince, of disturbances occurring within the Cheshire and inform you that your father has ordered that you, as the Earl of Chester must put an end to the said disturbances!"*

Edward the Black Prince replied, *"Thank you, Sir Harrow for passing on that vital information to me! Now, please return to my father and let him know that the problems currently besetting Cheshire shall be attended to! I and Henry of Grosmont, who is the Duke of Lancaster, are marching to Chester and we shall sort out the problems when we arrive there, we shall first find out what the underlying problems are, which are causing such disturbances among the people in the area.*

It seems to me that the people of my earldom would never disobey my commands for as long as they have just and fair treatment. Tell my father that the men of my earldom have offered to pay me a heavy fine if we bring the assize presently being held in Chester to an end. I wish you god speed and God be with you!" With that said, both men turned their horses and went their separate ways.

Although it seemed like Prince Edward had been successful in changing things, the justices opened an inquisition of trailbaston. (Trailbaston was a special type of itinerant judicial commission. The declared intention of which was to combat increasing levels of violence and public disorder but added bonuses for the crown of revenues which at times resulted in forfeiture.) This resulted in much money and property passing into the hands of Prince Edward, the 'Black Prince'.

Campaign at Aquitaine 1355 – 1364)

The father of the 'Black Prince' was King Edward III and he was determined to renew the war with France as he saw himself as the rightful heir to the French throne. Discussing the new coming invasion of France by English soldiers, King Edward III was speaking to the 'Black Prince'.

The king said, *"My son, England shall renew the war with the French! It is my divine right to rule both England and France! It is now the month of May of year 1355! I hereby order you and your army to invade Aquitaine while I act together with the king of*

Navarre in Normandy and the Duke of Lancaster upholds the cause of John of Montford in Brittany.

Your expedition has been made necessary because of the request of some of the Gascon Lords asking for your assistance and because they are eager to share in the plunder that shall be ours from fighting the French! Accordingly, I hereby appoint you as my lieutenant in Gascony and I authorise you to receive all homages due to England! You and your forces are to leave London for Plymouth on the 30th of June."

That resulted in the Black Prince and his forces getting to Plymouth and then having the frustration of being held up in that place because storms were making the voyage to France hazardous until the English fleet of three hundred ships finally set sail on the 8th of October. Present with the forces of the 'Black Prince' were Thomas Beauchamp, Earl of Warwick, William Ufford, Earl of Suffolk, William Montagu, Earl of Salisbury and John Vere, the Earl of Oxford.

Together with the over-all commander of the 'Black Prince', these men commanded one thousand men-at-arms, two thousand archers, and a very large contingent of Welsh infantry soldiers. Having arrived in France, the English force was received by the Cascon lords who received them with much rejoicing. Realising the necessity of the English soldiers to know what they were about to do, Edward, the 'Black Prince' addressed his assembled soldiers.

Prince Edward said, *"English soldiers and patriots, we are about to harry the French counties of Juliac, Armagnac, Comminges and then we cross over the Garonne at Sainte-Marie and Toulouse. Toulouse is occupied by a large force commanded by the John I, the Count of Armagnac! Our forces number fifteen hundred lancers, two thousand archers, and three thousand Light-at-foot infantry soldiers!"*

After that, the English soldiers were dismissed until required later. With that, Prince Edward and his army moved to Bordeaux, where they were enthusiastically received by the Gascon Lords who them with great rejoicing and celebration. After marauding and harrying the French areas near the Spanish border, the English army under the command of the 'Black Prince' did harry Juliac, Armagnac, Astrac and Comminges, they crossed the Garonne River, at Sainte-Marie, which was close to Toulouse.

That city was occupied by the count of Armagnac, John the 1st and his powerful force of soldiers. The defending count refused to let his soldiers sally forth to engage the Black Prince and his English army, choosing instead to maintain defence of the city.

That resulted in Edward the Black Prince by-passing Armagnac and moving on to the area of Lauragais. Arriving in that area, Prince Edward held an orders group and information was exchanged between the English soldiers. Having assembled his army in parade formations, Prince Edward addressed his men.

He said, *"Gentlemen, before us lies the town of Montgiscard and that is a position that our English army must take! There are many obstacles and French defences that English soldiers must overcome and it shall be a very difficult position for us to take, but take* it, we must! Our attack upon Montgiscard has to be ferocious and no quarter shall be given to our French enemies!

Although the defences are formidable, Montgiscard can and must be taken by English soldiers! In order to spur on the English efforts, I have authorised English soldiers to have a completely free hand in taking on and defeating the French! Our men are hereby permitted to rape the French women, and close with and kill as many French people as they want to! We are employing the principles of Total War to make the French give up the fight, therefore, you may kill, rape, and otherwise ill-treat the French population without any fear of disciplinary action from your English officers!

Also remember that the countryside in this part of France is very rich and fertile! Its people are good, hard-working, and simple people who are ignorant of war! Therefore, we must all fight hard and become completely victorious in Montgiscard and its surrounding towns and villages. There is great booty and spoils to be had by all English soldiers taking part in the glorious quest against the French!"

The English soldiers who were listening, became eager for the promised riches and booty to be had from the peaceful communities of that part of France. As a result, when the English attacked, they did so with great enthusiasm and ferocity, resulting in the English taking great spoil. Especially so, in the case of carpets, draperies, gold and jewels. The greedy English soldiers spared nothing and killed many men and children as well as raping many women and often killing them as well.

The only castle to resist the English was at Montgey. Its chatelaine (French title for the keeper of the castle) ordered his soldiers to help defend the castle by pouring beehives onto the oncoming English attackers. That was done and the English fled the scene in a panic when the bees were poured onto them!

Soon afterwards, Edward, the Black Prince called for his army to be given a series of orders groups until every English soldier knew and understood that England had to be victorious and that dire consequences threatened England if total victory was not quickly achieved. At the orders groups conducted on a unit and sub-unit basis for the entire English army, the commanders of the units and sub-units said, *"We are now going to attack Carcassonne! We shall not attack the citadel, which is too heavily defended, and we shall simply by-pass it. We are going to surround and lay siege to it. In time, it shall also fall!"*

So it was that Carcassonne was taken and sacked by the Black Prince and his army. Approaching Ormes near Narbonne, a single messenger bearing a white flag of truce was observed to be riding towards the English army by an alert English forward scout. He quickly and quietly informed his sub-unit commander, and he was told to intercept the messenger and to bring him before the Black Prince. That was done, and the messenger was taken to Prince Edward who spoke to the French messenger.

The Black Prince said, *"Well, messenger, what is it you have to tell me?"* The Frenchman replied, in French, *"Your majesty, as you already know, I am in the service of France generally and in particular, to Ormes! The people of Ormes and Trebes have authorised me to parley with you so that those two places can pay you to withdraw from this area and to leave both of the places alone! I am to return to the elders of both places with your demands as to what we must pay for you to leave us in peace! What answer shall I take back to my superiors, your majesty?"*

Edward, the Black Prince replied, *"Thank you for your efforts messenger! Please return to your people and let them know that I personally agree with what is being proposed for peace! However, I am only a prince, and the final decision is that of my father, King Edward III of England and it may take up to a month before we receive word of his will in this matter. Therefore, I cannot do anything until I have his answer. However, if the towns that you speak of were to swear allegiance to England and me, I could act on my father's behalf to accept what is being offer by both towns as long as the settlement in money terms is large enough! So, be sure to make the offer of the towns payment to England is extremely large! Now go and refresh before you return to the people who are waiting for your return in the two towns that you have mentioned!"*

The Black Prince next plundered Narbonne and during a pause in the fighting he was in conference with his officers. Addressing them he said, *"Gentlemen, some of you may already know that I was approached by a messenger from the Pope who wants us to allow him to begin negotiations for peace. I sent the messenger back to the Pope with the answer that I can do nothing util such times as I am informed about the will of my father, King Edward III of England! Gentlemen, the tactical situation is that we have the upper hand over the French and from Narbonne we are marching back to Bordeaux."*

As the English army was marching towards Bordeaux, it was observed by a forward scout of the army of the Count of Armagnac. The scout was taken before Count John I of Armagnac and he told the count what he had seen.

The count said, *"So, the English army is being led by the Black Prince and he is receiving much assistance from the Gascons and other French traitors! Very well, my army and I shall intercept him and destroy the English! Scout, go and refresh yourself! As soon as you have done so, you shall lead my army back to the English and we shall win!"*

Meanwhile, a small unit of the army of The Count of Armagnac became involved in heavy fighting with smaller English units and the French unit was suffering badly. It had many casualties including both dead and wounded soldiers from the encounter with the English near Toulouse. That caused the French unit to retreat into the city. That allowed the Black Prince to return to Bordeaux in triumph bringing with his army enormous amounts of the spoils of war. the whole English expedition lasted only eight weeks but resulted in the weakening of the French and a great amount of plunder being taken by the English.

Battle of Poitiers

Soon after awakening on the 6th of July 1356, the Black Prince (Edward) decided to set out on yet another expedition. He had the intention of marching through France to Normandy and upon arrival there, to give aid to his father's Norman allies, who were headed by the King of Navarre and Geoffrey d'Harcourt. He expected to be met by his father while there. Having called for an orders group among senior officers, the Black Prince said, *"Gentlemen, we shall cross the Dordogne at Bergerac on the 4th of August and then we shall move our army forwards through Auvergne, Limousin, and Berry! We shall be burning and plundering as we go! We shall do that until we come to Bourges where we shall burn the suburbs and attempt to take the city!"*

Edward, the Black Prince, and his army managed to burn the suburbs of Bourges, but they failed to take the city itself. Frustrated by the French resistance to the English attacks, Edward decided to attack Issoudun, which is a commune in the Indre department, and an administrative region of Centre-Val de Loire of France.

Meanwhile, the French King, John II, was organising the raising of a large force at Chartres from where he would be able to defend passages around the Loire and to send soldiers to fortresses in the areas which appeared to be in danger of imminent attack.

From Issoudun the Black Prince returned to his former line of attack and took Vierzon. While there, many scouting and intelligence gathering missions were conducted by the English army. The information that was gathered caused Edward to call an orders group. When the orders group was initiated, Edward addressed his officers.

He said, *"Gentlemen, I have been reliably informed that it shall not be possible for this army to cross the Loire or to form a junction with Lancaster and his army because he is now in Brittany! Accordingly, we shall return to Bordeaux via Poitiers! Before we leave this castle of Vierzon, we shall kill the defenders of that castle who have upset me by their sneaky ways and seemingly cowardly behaviour! We shall not have any mercy upon the French enemies because of the way they have conducted themselves!"* The reality of this being that the French defenders had fought bravely and hard. That resulted in more time than anticipated by the English to beat the garrison and as a result, the English wanted revenge.

On the 29th of August, Edward and his army marched towards Romorantin. While the English army was marching towards that place, it was attacked by a group of French knights who managed to inflict some casualties among the English. When he was informed of that, Edward, the Black Prince said, *"By God and his mother! Methinks that this situation must be immediately dealt with! I now need to speak to the scouts and other infantry members who have observed what the French are doing! Bring those English soldiers to me now, for I need to have their information!"*

That was organised, and the Black Prince was talking to private soldier Evans. He said, *"Private Evans, tell me all about the French who attacked us while we were marching towards Romorantin!"* Private Evens replied, *"Your majesty, I am one of your scouts! I and my second scout called Hobbs noticed that a group of five French knights and their men-at-arms were gathering intelligence about the English army. I informed my commanding officer, and he took action to engage the French in battle. That resulted in the Frenchmen fleeing after they had lost eleven of their men, who were dead! The remaining Frenchmen then fled into Romorantin, your majesty!"*

The Black Prince replied, *"Private soldier Evans, you have done well, and I thank you. Now return to your unit and prepare for further action! You have informed me that the French knights have fled to Romorantin, and it seems to me that this army must go there, because I would like the French knights to be nearer to us, in order to make it easier to kill them!"*

After that Prince Edward went out with the leading scouts of his army and saw for himself the fortress that was Romorantin. After personally inspecting the fortress, he sent out a demand for the fortress to surrender to him. Romorantin had Boucicault and other leaders as their defending officers. After these men rejected the demand to surrender from Edward, he assaulted the fortress on the 31st of August, and that resulted in him laying siege to it.

Enraged at the refusal of that place to surrender, Edward ordered, *"Line the launching buckets of our catapults with metal linings, thus making the launching buckets fire-proof by ling them with metal sheeting and bring the catapults into position! Gather large stones and rocks and cover them with both pitch and straw. When the catapults are in range and positioned correctly, set fire to the pitch and straw covered rocks, and launch them onto the roofs of the buildings in the enemy position!"*

That resulted in fire sweeping through the roofs of the buildings and Romorantin fell on the 3rd of September. On the 5th of September the English marched through Berry. Meanwhile the French King John II had assembled a large army and he went into pursuit of the English. When the French king was at Loches on the 12th of September he had twenty thousand men-at-arms. Using these, and his other forces he marched to Chauvigny and crossed the Vienne River.

At this time, the Black Prince and his army were marching parallel to the French, and they were only a few miles away from them. Due to the efforts of his scouts, the French king knew that Edward and his forces were at Chatellerault. He held an orders group with his senior commanding officers. He said, *"The English army at Chatellerault is advancing towards Poitiers and it must be stopped and wiped out!*

Tomorrow is Saturday the 14th of September, and you are to engage the English army in battle and wipe them out! We have a force of at least fifty thousand men-at-arms supported by archers and cavalry! You must outstrip the Black Prince who only has a force consisting of two thousand men-at-arms, supported by four thousand archers and one thousand five hundred light infantry. You do not have to worry about Edward getting help from Lancaster, because our armies have stopped him at Pont-de-Cé."

The Black Prince is Informed About the French Positions and Their Strength.

A knight who was wearing rather tired looking colours and armour, was escorted into the presence of Edward, the Black Prince. Upon seeing Edward, the knight raised his visor and spoke. He said, *"Your majesty, my men and I, along with other members of your army have been skirmishing with some advanced French units. Accordingly, our army has taken up positions on the rising high ground to the south-east of Miausson and the old Roman road near La Cardinerie, which is a farming commune near Beauvior. Our force shall remain there overnight at least. We know that the French significantly outnumber our English forces, but due to us having the high ground and better strategic positions we can win against them! That is also known by the French king, otherwise why would he send a cardinal to make peace with you?*

Also, tomorrow we are supposed to hold a meeting with Cardinal Hélie Talleyrand of Périgord who has been appointed by King John II of France to make peace, if possible! What answer do you wish me to take back to the French king, your majesty?"

The Black Prince replied, *"Tell the cardinal and the French king that I am willing to confer about terms. In order to establish peace, I am willing to give up all of the towns and castles which I have taken and to set free all French prisoners-of-war! Also, if King John II of France makes peace, I shall not serve against France for a period of seven years! If the French do not immediately agree, the war shall continue, because it appears to me that the French are suffering badly, and they shall fail!"*

Those decisions and demands by the English 'Black Prince' were dismissed by the French after King John II had been advised not to accept the English offer of peace and terms. Instead, the French King demanded, *"The Black Prince of England and at least one hundred of his knights must surrender themselves to my French forces, or no peace can exist between France and England!"*

Meanwhile, the cardinal kept up his negotiating for peace between the warring parties. His negotiations were protracted and in the interest of the French as the French side was playing for time so that they could bring re-inforcements into play and so destroy the little English army.

King John II allowed the English time off from fighting because it was Sunday. That turned out to be a mistake! The English front was covered in vines and hedges, providing good hiding places for archers to be positioned out of sight of the French. On the left side of the English, and to their rear, was the Miausson Ravine and much broken ground. The right-side flank was the woods and the Abbey of Nouaillé. All day, the English soldiers were busy digging trenches and making fences, resulting it now being a well-entrenched camp, just as the English had been at Crecy.

Price Edward formed up his army into three divisions. The first being commanded by the Earls of Warick and Suffolk. The second division was commanded by Edward and the third located in the rear, being commanded by Salisbury and Oxford. The French had four divisions which were placed one behind the other. That lost them the advantage of their greater numbers of soldiers because the French first line was exposed to its front and its sides to the hidden English archers who had with them three hundred men-at-arms. That allowed the English force to ambush the French as they moved along the narrow front to try and engage the English.

At the break of day of the 19th of September, the Black Prince spoke to his little army and afterwards, the fight began. Meanwhile, on the French side, a senior French officer was speaking to his sub-ordinates. He said, *"Gentlemen, I need you to organise three hundred volunteers who are extremely good men-at-arms to ride through the English position to the front of us and wipe out the English!'* That was done and when the Frenchmen approached the English position the English archers shot them down!

Suddenly, a loud command came from the English side. An English knight ordered, *"English men-at-arms, mount your horses and charge the Frenchmen near the bottom of the hill! You have the high ground, so that means the downhill momentum created by your charge will scatter the French!"* The Black Prince shouted to his banner bearer, *"English banners, advance in the name of God and his mother and Saint George!"* that resulted the French not being able to withstand the English charge and so, the Frenchmen fled in disorder!

The next French division under the command of the Phillip the Duke of Orleans also fled the battlefield. In the French rear, the French King, John II was fighting in person with great gallantry. The English actions resulted in the utter defeat of the French. The fighting had lasted until mid-afternoon, and the battlefield was littered with eleven thousand dead French soldiers. As well, up to two thousand French soldiers were made prisoners. King John II and his son, Phillip were among those taken prisoner. The English losses were small.

The Black Prince Receives John II

When King John II of France was brought before him, Prince Edward received him with respect. He helped the French king remove his armour him and many French princes and barons were given a dinner and were praised by their English captors. The following day, Price Edward began the return journey to Bordeaux, expecting problems caused by French units along the way. However, the English were not attacked, and the French king and his son remained prisoners of the English.

Marriage of the Black Prince on 10 October 1361

Now aged thirty-one years, Edward the Black Prince courted and married Joan, the Countess of Kent on the 10th of October 1361. She was born on the 29th of September 1327. She was known as *'The Fair Maid of Kent'* and she the daughter of Edmund of Woodstock. Edmund was always a loyal supporter of his elder half-brother, King Edward II and that placed him at odds with Isabella, the king's wife.

His courtship of Joan began when Edward, the Black Prince had been actively fighting the French and he was attracted to Joan. So it was, that he presented her with a silver cup, which had been taken as booty from the French by him. He was three years younger than her.

Speaking to his father King Edward III about his desire for her, the Black Prince said, *"My father, I desire to marry Joan the Countess of Kent, but she has a complicated marital record which could be easily misinterpreted by others. I think that I need you input about this Father!"*

King Edward III said, *"My son, I shall always back you up in all that you do. In order to get this marriage of yours approved by the people of England, it makes perfect sense for us to inform the Pope of the situation and to get his approval and dispensation."*

So it was that not only did the current Pope grant his dispensation for the Black Prince and the Countess of Kent to marry, but that was also carried on by his successor, Pope Innocent VI. At the king's request, four such dispensations were granted.

Barely nine months after the death of her previous husband, when Joan, the countess of Kent and Edward, the Black Prince were married on the 10th of October 1361 at Windsor Castle. Both King Edward III and his wife were present at the wedding which was celebrated by the Archbishop of Canterbury.

In 1362, the Black Prince was invested as the Prince of Aquitaine. He and Joan moved to the town of Bordeaux where they spent the next nine years. During that time, they had two sons born to them. Their eldest son was Edward of Angoulême, who died at the age of five. During the birth of their youngest son, the future King Richard II, the Black Prince received a letter asking him for help from King Peter of Castile.

Edward responded by giving Peter the aid he had asked for and that resulted the achievement of one of his greatest victories. King Peter was killed and that resulted in no money to pay the soldiers. In the meantime, the wife of the Black Prince was forced to raise another army because her husband's enemies were threatening Aquitaine during his absence.

Prince of Aquitaine & Gascony

On the 19th of July 1362, King Edward III held a grand celebration because his son, Prince Edward, also known as the 'Black Prince', was installed into the position of, and given the title of *'Prince of Aquitaine and Gascony'* by him. King Edward had decided the regions would be held as a principality and held by his son, and that the Black Prince would pay an ounce of gold per year as the price of paying homage to his father and England.

After Christmas, he and his wife received his father Edward III, and his wife at his court at Berkhamsted and after enjoying a family Christmas with his father, Edward, the Black Prince, and his wife called Joan sailed with their household for Gascony and landed at La Rochelle.

There, he was met by John Chandos, the king's Lieutenant. After that he proceeded with John Chandos to Poitiers where he received homage from the lords of Poitou and Saintonge. After that the Black Prince rode to various cities until he arrived at Bordeaux and received homage paid to him by the lords of Gascony. In order to made the administration of that part of France easier, he lived and held his court, sometimes at Bordeaux and sometimes at Angoulême.

Edward, the Black Prince next appointed John Chandos as the constable of Guyenne and gave the knights of his household with profitable offices. That resulted in those knights keeping a lot of state and spending extravagantly. Their extravagance displeased many people. Many of the Gascon lords objected to becoming vassals of the English, and that compounded the dissatisfaction felt by many of these French lords who were now subjects of the English Prince.

After the English had displayed that they were living in their opulent luxury, the feelings of dissatisfaction greatly increased. Arnaud Amanieu who was the lord of Albret and many others were always ready to give whatever help they could to the French cause. As well, Gaston, the Count of Foix was aiding the French cause in secret. He had visited the Black Prince on his first arrival and then gave him trouble in 1365 by refusing to pay homage for Bearn.

The French crown passed on to Charles V, in April 1364, and Charles carefully encouraged the malcontents within the English possessions of Aquitaine and Gascony. These things combined and the position of the English 'Black Prince' was not easy to maintain.

Things remained quiet until April of 1363, when Prince Edward found that he was required to mediate between the Counts of Foix and Armagnac, who had been at war with each other for some time. Next, he also tried to mediate between Charles of Blois and John Montford, who were the rival competitors. Both of these men appeared before him and although he tried to mediate between them, he was unsuccessful.

During May of 1363, the Black Prince of England received and entertained King Peter of Cyprus at Angoulême where he was holding a tournament. After a while, the war in Brittany was resumed. That led the Black Prince to appoint Chandos to lead an army to help out Montfort, resulting in Chandos winning the Battle of Auray against the French on the 29th of September 1364. Prince Edward spoke to John Chandos.

He said, *"Look here John, I keep on getting complaints about the ravages of serving English forces ravaging various parts of Gascony and other parts of France! Although I am not forbidding you and the other* leaders of the English free companies from ravaging the French, I hereby call upon you and the others to apply restraint your ravages! After all, I do not want my subjects in Aquitaine and Gascony to rise against us!"

Spanish Campaign 1365-1367)

In 1365 the free companies commanded by Sir Hugh Calveley and other leaders, served with Bertrand du Guesclin, who employed them in making King Peter of Castile flee from his kingdom and to set-up his bastard brother, Henry of Trastamara in his stead.

King Peter called his messengers. When they arrived, he spoke to them. He said, *"Greetings to you, my loyal messengers! I have an important message for you to take to my ally King Edward III of England and his son, Edward the Black Prince who is also the Prince of Aquitaine and Gascony! The message is written on this parchment which also has my royal seal on its container. No-one is to open the container and the message must be delivered to both King Edward III of England and to his son, the Black Prince of Aquitaine and Gascony. That is why you shall operate as two teams of ten men. Two of you shall be messengers, while the eight other members shall form the escorts for each team. Now go and deliver these messengers to the two men who are my close allies".*

That was done and upon arrival at Windsor Castle where King Edward III was staying, the messengers approached the English King. Their leader said, *"Yor majesty, I am Jose, a messenger in the service of your ally King Peter of Castile! I have a sealed container with the message inside of it!"* King Edward III said, *"Very well messenger, you may open the sealed container and then read the message to me. I have had a full day of reading and making judgements and I do not wish to read any more today!"*

Joshe replied, *"Very well your majesty."* And he then opened the container and took out the message. Next, he read out the message to King Edward. He said, *"King Edward, I am Peter of Castile, your great friend and ally! I have been stripped of my kingdom and my bastard half-brother has been put into power in my place. I implore you and your son, Edward, the Black Prince to come to my aid and to re-install me as the king of my country!"*

Having heard the message read out to him, Edward said, *So, my friend and ally Peter of Castile has had his throne usurped by his bastard brother! I shall not abide with this! Messenger, you are to travel to where my son is in Aquitaine with my written orders for him to assist King Peter of Castile!"* As usual, two copies of this order shall be made. One to be taken to my son, and the other one shall be kept on file. You are to refresh yourself and rest while the documents are being prepared. As soon as they are ready, you and your escort shall depart for Bordeaux!"

However, many of the lords of the Black Prince did not want to fight for the cause of Peter or for that matter another foreign king. King Edward III declared, *"It is not fitting that a bastard should inherit a kingdom or drive or attempt to drive out his lawfully installed bother, further-more no king or any son of a king should suffer such disrespect to loyalty! Not only that, but there must be no person to attempt to turn me, King Edward III of England away from my determination to restore the King of Castile!"*

Meanwhile, King Peter of Castile won friends through his declaration about the Black Prince. King Peter said, *"Let it be known by all of those people here today that I intend to make the son of the English King Edward III, the king of Galicia, and that I shall divide my riches among those who help me!"*

An English Parliament was held at Bordeaux, and it decided to ask King Edward III about his desires to help King Peter regain his throne. Answering the question, King Edward said, *"I refer to my earlier comments about this matter! I said then, and I also say now, that it is right and proper for my son, Edward whom you all know as the 'Black Prince' to help King Peter! See to it that what I have said and ruled upon in this matter is put into a letter and taken to my son in Bordeaux!"*

Another parliament was held by the Black Prince at Bordeaux at which the letter containing the words of King Edward III were read out. That resulted in the reluctant English and Gascon lords agreeing to give their help to both the Black Prince and King Peter of Castile, provided that their pay was secured to them. Edward, the Black Prince stated, *"I am appearing before you, my lords to re-assure you that your money payments are safe! In order to give you all security, I hereby agree to lend King Peter whatever money is required, now go back to your units and rest comfortably knowing that I, Prince Edward, the Prince of Wales, Aquitaine and Gascon shall be backing you up and paying for what King Peter may not be able to do!"* That had the desired effect and so, the lords agreed to help.

The Black Prince and King Peter than held a conference with Charles of Navarre which resulted in the Black Prince making a payment of fifty-six thousand florins as a loan to King Peter who then paid that sum to Charles of Navarre which allowed the Black Prince to be in possession of the province of Biscay and the fortress of Castro de Urdiales as pledges for the repayment of the debt owing to the Black Prince and England.

Prince Edward received a hundred thousand francs from his father King Edward III, and that was part of the ransom paid for the late King John II of France. While his army was still assembling, the Black Prince remained at Angoulême where he was visited by king Peter. He then went to Bordeaux where he spent Christmas with his wife, Joan, and she gave birth to his second son, called Richard. (The next King of England).

After Calveley and other English and Gascon leaders found out that the Black Prince was about to fight for King Peter, they withdrew their services to Henry of Trastamara and joined Edward, the Black Prince saying, *"We are in your service because you are the Black Prince and our natural lord!"*

Prince Edward left Bordeaux during early February of 1367 and joined his army at Dax. He remained there for the next three days, during which time he received re-inforcements from his father, King Edward III. The re-inforcements he got were four hundred men-at-arms and an additional four hundred archers, who were under the command of his brother John, the Duke of Lancaster.

From Dax the Black Prince marched via Saint-Jean-Pied-de-Port, through Roncesvalles in the Pyrenees to Pamplona which was the capital of Navarre. While still at Pamplona, Prince Edward received a letter of defiance from Henry of Trastamara.

The letter stated, *"Prince Edward of England, you and your minions have invaded my lands which I find to be irksome and the presence of you and your English army to be an offence against the dignity of myself and my people! I and my people want you uncultured heavens from the barbaric nation called England to leave all areas which you have occupied in Spain and France because you are just foreign heavens who are unwanted and who have no legitimate business here! So, pack up and leave before you and your men find yourselves in difficult situations because of your ambition and your greed! Just leave!"*

Signed Henry of Trastámara. Under that was his wax seal.

From Pamplona the Black Prince marched his army via Arruiz to Salvaterra. That city opened its gates to the English army and welcomed the Englishmen. That allowed the Black Prince and his men to rest before they advanced to Vitoria. Arriving there, Prince Edward called for an orders group to be held. When the meeting took place, Edward, the Black Prince addressed his officers.

He said, *"Gentlemen, I have received a letter of defiance from Henry of Trastámara and he has made it plain that he is our enemy so we must carefully watch what he and his forces are doing!*

That brings me to our next task! Before we can go on to Burgos by direct route, we must carefully reconnoitre the route lest we are ambushed while we march along it! After Burgos this army must take highly defensible positions held by Henry! They include Santo Domingo de la Calzada which is to the right of the River Ebro.

If it turns out that we cannot reach Burgos through Alava, we shall cross the Ebro and camp under the walls of Logrono. The reconnoitre force shall be one made up of seven knights and all of their men-at-arms! The reconnoitre force shall be commanded by Sir William Felton. It shall draw its supplies and provisions and then leave in order to fulfil the reconnoitre immediately! So, unless some of you have questions or do not yet understand your orders, to all of your duties fall out!"

That was followed by Sir William Felton and his knights and their men-at-arms collecting their supplies and then moving out to complete the reconnoitre as the Black Prince required! A forward scout of the English named John Cummins conferred with his second scout. John said, *"Look over there towards the east, William, I can see a large skirmishing party which I think it will be for the best to avoid!"*

William looked towards the east and he said, *"Yes John, I agree that we should not let the enemy know that we are here because they out-number us significantly! All the same, we must inform our superior officers of this!"*

And so, the two scouts of the English reconnoitre party sought out Sir William Felton and reported to him. John Cummins approached Sir William Felton and raised his visor in salute. He said, *"Sir, There is a very large skirmishing party which appears to be on the side of the enemy, Henry of Trastámara approaching this unit from the east! The enemy unit outnumbers our unit in significant strength! What are your orders, sir?"*

Sir William Felton replied, *"Never let it be said that the English army runs away from a fight with the lessor enemy forces! You, Private soldier John Cummins will ride back to the main body of the English army at Arruiz and inform the Black Prince that we have engaged the skirmishing force of Henry in battle! Now, to your new duties fall out!"* that was followed by Sir William Felton and all of his reconnoitre force being defeated by the skirmishing force of Henry of Trastámara.

As Henry held Santo de la Calzada the Black Prince was forced to cross the Ebro and then camp under the walls of Logrono as it had been thought could happen. During that time, the Black Prince's army was suffering from the lack of supplies for both its men and its horses. As well, the English soldiers were suffering from the wet weather and the accompanying wind. Still, having refuge in Logrono, the English were better off.

On the 30th of March 1367, Prince Edward wrote an answer to Henry's letter to him. He wrote, *"You and your lot are simply traitors to King Peter! King Peter has told me that you are a traitor and that he shall deal harshly with you!"*

At twilight of the morning of the 3rd of April, Edward the Black Prince and his army marched from Navarrete, and everyone dismounted while the English were still a great distance from Henry's army. Being at the head of his army, Edward the Black Prince decided that it was time for him to encourage his soldiers and that was most easily done by the use of propaganda.

As all of the English army had dismounted, the Black Prince again mounted his horse and moved to a hilltop so that he could easily be seen and heard over great distances. Then, just as the sun appeared over the horizon, he was silhouetted and plainly visible to everyone. All of a sudden, he very loudly prayed.

He shouted, *"Lord my God, My heavenly father, here we are, the army of England commanded by your faithful servant Prince Edward, of England! We are here at Najera to put right the wrongs inflicted upon the King of Castile called Peter by his bastard brother who has unjustly usurped his throne from him! I beseech you my Lord and God to aid my English army to achieve total victory over Henry today! Lord God, please send a fright into the evil enemies who oppose us because they are in league with Satan!"*

Edward then spoke to King Peter. He said, *"Well, Peter, you have heard me implore god to aid us in obtaining total victory over your brother Henry who is a bastard and who has taken away your throne by devious means! We have with us archers armed with English longbows as well as three thousand lancers. You enemies will rue the day they tried to battle you and your friends from England!"*

Overhead, the sky began to darken as clouds quickly built up to thunderheads hanging low in the sky and they had the effect of darkening the countryside to the point where many men were feeling uneasy, and they thought that the weather was threatening them! A few moments later, rain began to fall as thunder built up and lightening flashed across the sky.

King Peter of Castile said, *"Thank you Edward, that was a fine and rousing speech you made while loudly praying to God for Victory over Henry and his forces! Now, it would seem that God has heard your prayer to him, and he has sent this weather to aid you and to punish my half-brother!"* Edward just smiled and then he ordered, *"Banners, march towards the enemy in the name of Saint George and God to help English do what is right!*

You can see the low ground in front of you! When you get much closer to the enemy, turn from the enemy and run back towards our English line! That will made the enemy chase after you and that you can then lead the enemy to where our archers and lancers are waiting for them!

That in turn will enable those men to close with and kill the enemy! English Lancers, mount up and ride to the top of his hill and the next one near it! You must possess the high ground! Archers, one thousand of you shall accompany the Lancers to the hilltops. When the enemy comes into sight, use your English longbows to rain death upon the enemy ranks."

Meanwhile, Edward's allies, the Gascon lords attacked the flanks of the main body of Henry's army, and they were successful. At much the same time the vanguard of Henry's army tried to chase after fleeing English, only to be cut down by the intense barrages of arrows and charges of the lancers who were charging down the hills they occupied. Next, the Black Prince brought the main body of his army into action resulting in total defeat of Henry's forces who fled from the battlefield.

With the battle now over, Edward the Black Prince spoke to King Peter. He said, *"Peter, we have well and truly beaten your brother Henry and his forces! I now ask you to forgive those who have wronged you and to spare their lives!"* King Peter of Castile said, *"Yes Edward, I shall do as you ask and spare their lives with the exception of a notorious traitor whom I shall personally kill now and two others who shall die by my hand on the next morning! Thank you, my ally, for providing me with such tremendous assistance! Your father Edward III of England must be very proud of you!"*

Among the French prisoners was marshal Arnoul d'Audrehem. He had formerly been a prisoner of the Black Prince and Prince Edward released him after d'Audrehem gave him his word that he would not bear arms again. That caused Prince Edward to say, *"Get away from me you disgusting liar who has no honour! Go on, go away, and hang your head in the shame of what you are, a liar and coward! I do not wish to see you again! You shall face a trial by your peers who are all knights!"*

Burgos

On the 5th of April 1367, Edward the Black Prince and King Peter of Castile marched to Burgos, where they celebrated Easter. Edward, did not take up lodgings within the city, choosing instead to camp outside of the walls of the monastery of Las Huelgas.

King Peter of Castile did not pay Prince Edward the money that he owed him. That resulted in Edward, the Black Prince showing some exasperation. So, the Prince Edward said, *"I remind you of the solemn renewal of the oath which you made in public on the 23rd of September 1367 in which you stated before the people and before God that you shall pay me the money that you owe me! I also remind you that you made the original oath to repay me according to the terms of my loan agreement to you at the high alter of the cathedral of Burgos.*

I am not impressed by the way that you are attempting to get out of repaying your loan from England and me! Not only that, but you have proven yourself to me to be a liar and a thief! I can plainly see that you have no intention of repaying the money that my father and I have lent to you! That being the case, I hereby demand that that you grant me your province of Biscay and be quick about it, because I suspect that you have no intention of ever paying your debts and that I may have to deal with you using the armed force and might of my combined English and Gascon army! I warn you, King Peter of Castile, that my patience is running out and when it does you shall lose everything!"

King Peter had no intention of ever repaying the Back Prince, but he knew that he was courting disaster by offending him. Therefore, Peter decided to get rid of his creditor. So, he said, *"Edward, these are the facts. Firstly, I cannot get the money owed to you at Burgos. There is much more money to be had at Seville and I shall send you the money owed if you wait for it to arrive at Valladolid.*

Secondly, You must not venture into the province of Biscay because the people will not allow you to tell them what and what not to do within their own country!"

That resulted in Prince Edward and his army taking up lodgings at Valladolid and waiting there in vain for the promised money payments. While Prince Edward and his army were at Valladolid, there was a lot of hot weather and a very large part of the Black Prince's army suffered from dysentery. Things were so bad that only one out of every five Englishmen returned to England. The Black Prince himself suffered from that disease and he never fully recovered from it. Some people think that the ill health of the Black Prince's army was caused by poison!

While that was happening, Henry of Trastámara was invading Aquitaine and making war upon its population. Having taken Bagnéres, Henry wasted the countryside of Aquitaine. Meanwhile, after having successfully negotiated safe passage through his lands with King Peter of Aragon, the Black Prince and his army passed through that territory and reached Bordeaux via Roncesvalles during early February of 1367.

War in Aquitaine 1366 – 1370

When the Black Prince was gathering his army for his Spanish expedition, the lord of Albret agreed to serve the Black Prince with a thousand lancers. However, because of limited food supplies, Edward the Black Prince wrote to him and requested him to only come with two hundred lancers. That upset the lord of Albret, and peace was only restored when his uncle made peace between him and the Black Prince. Meanwhile, the French King Charles, offered Albret a pension and as a result, drew the lord of Albret and his uncle into the French side.

During the spring of 1370, Charles raised two large armies to invade Aquitaine. The first one was under the command of Louis I, the Duke of Anjou, while the other army was commanded by John, the Duke of Berry, who was to march towards Limousin and join with the first army commanded by Louis I. After their uniting of both armies, they were to besiege the Black Prince who was in Angoulême.

An English sentry went to where the Black Prince was lying in his bed because of the weakness caused by his dysentery. He said, *"I am sorry to have to bother you while you are recovering from your illness your majesty, but all English soldiers have need of your presence in the field now that the French are attacking!"*

Prince Edward left his bed and proceeded to gather an army at Cognac, and he was joined at that place by the barons of Poitou and Saintonge. He was also joined by the English Earls of Cambridge, Lancaster, and Pembroke. During that time, the two French armies had united and had successfully taken many English held cities. They also laid siege to Limoges which was treacherously surrendered to the French by Bishop Jean de Murat de Cros. That was made even harder to bear by the Black Prince because the bishop had *supposedly* been one of his trusted friends.

Shortly prior to that, during mid-morning, a messenger was escorted to Prince Edward. The Black Prince said, *"Yes, messenger, what is it that you must tell me?"* The messenger replied, *"Your majesty, I bear the alarming news that your friend, the Bishop Jean de Murat de Cros has surrendered Limoges to the French enemy!"*

Prince Edward was stunned by the news. After a while, he recovered his composure and spoke. He said, *"I hereby swear upon the soul of my grandfather that I shall retake Limoges soon!"* Next, he spoke directly to the messenger. He said, *"Messenger, you have done well! Now go and eat, have some water and some rest before you resume your duties. You are now excused!"*

Prince Edward and his army marched toward the French enemy. Due to him suffering badly from his illness, the black Prince was unable to ride and therefore he was carried on a litter, and he directed the action against the French from his litter. He set out with a small army of almost four thousand men. Seeing Limoges in the distance, Prince Edward called for an orders group with his senior officers. When they all attended, he said, *"Gentlemen, it is now high time for us English to encircle and lay siege to Limoges! As soon as you have encircled the city, you are to send me our English army engineering commanders! I have important and urgent work for them! Now return to your units and get this attack under way! To your duties, fallout!"*

A short time later, two English engineering Officers reported for duty to the Black Prince. They were escorted to where he was lying on his litter. As they approached, he said, *"Yes, gentlemen, what is it?"* The two engineering officers replied, *"Your majesty, we are two of your engineering officers. We have been ordered to appear before you!"*

Prince Edward replied, *"Thank you my loyal soldiers! As you know, we are at war in this place because the bishop here pretended to be a friend of England and instead of helping us English, he surrendered the city to the French! Therefore, we must retake Limoges immediately! You are to work toward undermining sections of the city's walls so that we can then successfully launch an assault into Limoges. Today is the 17th of September and I need at least a section of* *the city's walls to come down on the 19th of September. Can you, do it?"*

Both of the engineering officers said, *"Yes, your majesty, we should be able to do that. We shall return to our units and begin to have our men working on undermining the wall at it most critical point, near where the river bends!"* That was successfully accomplished and the two engineering officers than caused the ditch to be filled with the rubble and other material that came from the ruins of the wall's section. As the section of the walls of Limoges came down, the English men-at-arms who were waiting just outside of the wall, rushed in and stormed the city, causing much destruction and a great loss of life among the French people there.

The Black Prince was carried into Limoges on his stretcher by his soldiers and placed upon a rampart on a wall so that he could see what was happening below him in the city. Bishop Jean de Murat de Cros was brought before him, and present was the Duke of Lancaster.

When he saw the bishop, the Black Prince was filled with loathing, and he ordered that the bishop immediately was to be killed by cutting off his head. Unexpectedly, the Duke of Lancaster objected to that, and the English soldiers then pillaged the city and massacred up to three thousand people of all ages and occupations. After that, the Black Prince returned to Cognac and his illness increased. As a result, he was not able to take part in further operations with his army. He finally went to Angoulême and then on to Bordeaux.

Return to England

Meanwhile, the son of Edward the Black Prince who was called Edward of Angoulême, died in 1371 and that caused the Black Prince very much grief. His health continued to get worse, and his personal doctor advised him to return to England. He discussed the matter with Joan and Lancaster and then returned to England, landing at Southampton during January of 1371. He met his father, Edward III at Windsor.

During that meeting, he said to King Edward III, *"My father, you must put a stop to that treaty you have made with Charles of Navarre! If that actually goes ahead, England shall have to cease to have lands there just because the French upstart demands it! I do not like that at all and it must be stopped from happening!"* After that Prince Edward returned to his manor in Berkhamsted.

After staying there for a while, the Black Prince went out into the English countryside and while there, he spoke to many people from the communities. He was immediately recognised as a leading opponent of the influence that was exercised by the anti-clerical Lancastrian party and he was trusted by the clergy, many of whom looked to him for leadership.

So it was that Friar Irving Berkenstead came to him. Upon the exchange of niceties being dealt with, the friar spoke to the Black Prince. He said, *"My Lord Prince Edward, I am here to offer you the services of my superiors who are awaiting your answer at Canterbury Cathedral!"*

The Black Prince replied, *"Thank you, Friar, for pointing this out! Please return to your superiors at Canterbury and let them know that I shall protect them from those who wish to do the Church ill! In order for me to be able to do that and to continue protecting the Church, I want the Church leaders to meet and convene a convocation of the Canterbury Church leaders at the Savoy on the 2nd of May 1372. Also tell them to discuss the possibility of them making an exceptionally large grant and all shall be well!"*

The health of the Black Prince began to improve and in August of 1372 he joined his father in sailing to France to relieve Thouars. However, contrary wind meant that the English fleet did not reach the cost of France. On October the 6th he resigned as the Prince of Aquitaine and Gascony. His reasons being that the revenues of those places were not sufficient to cover costs. He acknowledged his resignation at the Parliament of the following month and after its conclusion, and after the knights had been dismissed, he met the citizens and conferred with them. He said, *"My people, I, Prince Edward who most of you know as the Black Prince, hereby ask you and prevail upon you to extend the customs which you granted the year before this one to protect merchant shipping for another year!"*

On the 20th of May 1374, a letter from Pope Gregory XI was read out to a council of prelates and nobles which was presided over by Prince Edward. The letter was demanding that England pay him a subsidy to help him against the Florentines. The bishops, after hearing the letter being read to them, agreed that the

Pope was correct in demanding money from England to enable the Church to fight its enemies and they pressed the English nobility for support. However, Prince Edward did not share that view and he wanted the cause of the English crown to be maintained.

During a debate with bishops, Prince Edward spoke. He said, *"Archbishop Whittlesey! You have provided no good ideas or debate! You are simply sitting upon your fat arse and doing very little! The cause of the crown of England shall be vigorously maintained and we shall not send money or military aid to Pope Gregory XI or to his Lord-in-chief John! Archbishop, it is my considered opinion that you are an ass!"* The bishops then gave way, and it was declared, *"Lord-in-chief' John of the Vatican has no power to bring the kingdom of England and its people into subjugation! England shall take part in the wars of the Vatican!"*

Before and during the meeting of the 'Good Parliament of the 28th of April 1376, he was seen as the main support of the common people who were attacking the abuses of the administration, acting in concert with William of Wykeham in opposing the influence of Lancaster and the disreputable bunch of courtiers who wanted to uphold it. Towards the middle of that Parliament, the Prince's illness returned in force.

Death of Edward the Black Prince

Even from about the middle of the Good Parliament, Prince Edward knew that he was dying. The dysentery that he was suffering from became so violent, that he occasionally fainted from weakness. He was visited by his father who came to see him after he was told that Edward had died. That was not yet the case, and the two men spoke.

The Black Prince said, *"My father, I am weak from the effects of dysentery, and I shall now take this opportunity to say goodbye to you! I almost died a few days ago and my doctor has told me that I may not have long to live! Father, I must ask you to confirm the gifts for my servants that are detailed in my will, and I implore you to settle all of my outstanding debts out of my estate and that you protect my son Richard!"*

King Edward III left his son's manor house with a heavy heart. The death of his son, the Black Prince was announced on the 8th of June 1376. He was buried in the Canterbury Cathedral on the 29th of September. His epitaph is inscribed around his effigy reads:

Such as thou art, sometime was I.

Such as I am, such shalt thou be.

I thought little on th'our of death.

So long as I enjoyed breath.

On earth I had great riches

Land, houses, great treasure,

Horses money and gold.

But now a wretched captive am I,

Deep in the ground, lo here I lie,

My beauty great, is all quite gone,

My flesh is wasted to the bone.

Joan's Transition to Dowager Princess of Wales

Prior to that, due to his poor health, the Black Prince was no longer able to perform his duties as Prince of Aquitaine and that resulted in he and his wife Joan returning to England soon after they had buried their eldest son in 1371. During the following year of 1372, the black Prince forced himself to attempt to save his father's possessions in France. However, the exertion completed the ill health and disruption to his body caused by his dysentery, from which he never fully recovered.

The second son of Joan and Edward the Black Prince was now in line to succeed his grandfather, Edward III. Edward III died on 21st of June 1377. Soon afterwards, the ten-year-old Richard was crowned as King Richard II. In the early years of his reign, he faced the Peasants' Revolt. The religious reformers called Lollards were led by John Wycliff who had enjoyed Joan's support. However, the violent climax of the popular movement for reform reduced the normally feisty Joan to a woman who was terrorised.

As the mother of the king, Joan found that she exercised lots of influence behind the scenes and she was recognised for her contributions during the reign of her son. She had respect among people who saw her as a royal dowager. Returning to London from visiting the shrine of Thomas A' Becket at Canterbury Cathedral, she found her way barred by a rebel. Reverting to her true self, she indignantly spoke aloud! She said, *"Get out of my way, you low grade person! I am the dowager*

Princess of Wales Joan, whom you may know of as the wife of the Black Prince, and we have aided your cause many times!"

That prompted the rebel who was barring her way to speak. He said, *"This is the revolt of the Peasants, and we shall not take any heed of the likes of you!"* That was overheard by Wat Tyler, the leader of the revolt. He came forward and he recognised her.

Having done so, he loudly spoke to all people. He said, *"Shame upon all of you! This lady is in fact one of the greatest benefactors we have! This is the Dowager Princess of Wales called Joan, the wife of the Black Prince who has been a supporter of all of you! Not only shall you let her through, but you shall escort her, and you will see to it that no harm becomes her! Is that clear?"* The result was that she was escorted through the mob and while she was doing so, she was saluted with people blowing her kisses and given an escort to help her complete the rest of her journey in safety.

Summary

No matter what some people may say about Isabella, the fact remains that due to many provocations, she deposed her husband, King Edward II and replaced him with her and Edward's son who became King Edward III. He, in turn became the king who made a renaissance of the English language happen by decreeing that only English be used in all matters before English courts rather than the continued use of French. Edward III began the One Hundred

Years war with France because he coveted the French Crown.

He married, and his eldest son, also called Edward, was the Black Prince who did much to restore English pride and like his father, was considered to be the epitome of English chivalry and knighthood. His son, Richard went on to become king in his own right, but that is another story.

Bibliography

Warner, Katherine, (24th of May 2016) *Isabella of France: The Rebel Queen.* Amazon & Amberly Publishing.

Buescher, Michael, (2008) *The Fitzalans: Earls of Arundle & Surrey Lords of the Marshes.* Glasgow Logaston Press.

Murison, A.F., (2014) *King Robert the Bruce* Penman Press

Lacey, Robert, (2011), *Great Tales from English History.* Little, Brown, London.

Barber, Richard, (January 2008), *"Edward Prince of Wales & Aquitaine: A biography of the Black Prince.* Alan Lane, London.

Barber, Richard, (2004), *Joan Suo jure countess of Kent & Princess of Wales,* Oxford University Press.

Laune, Penny, (2015) *Joan of Kent: the first Princess of Wales.* Amberly Publishing, Gloucestershire.

Isabella Warrior Queen

www.ingramcontent.com/pod-product-compliance
Lightning Source LLC
Chambersburg PA
CBHW070532090426
42735CB00013B/2950